HEART BOSS

Rooting for you to
let your heart
be boss.

♡.

Regan

Rooting for you to
let your heart
be boss.

♡

Taylor

HEART BOSS

Trust Your Gut,
Shed Your Shoulds, and
Create a Life You Love

REGAN WALSH

HOUNDSTOOTH
PRESS

HEART BOSS
Trust Your Gut, Shed Your Shoulds, and Create a Life You Love

ISBN   978-1-5445-1873-2   *Hardcover*
       978-1-5445-1872-5   *Paperback*
       978-1-5445-1871-8   *Ebook*

To Dorothy and Maeve,
May your big, beautiful hearts always be the boss of you.
I love you.

—Mom

Heart Boss

The world is made of a thousand voices.
Yet, even at midnight, at the bottom
of the canyon, at the edge of the forest,
in the belly of the sky, I hear you.

Speak to me in the old language—
in the wisdom of throb and churn,
the power of thump and pulse.

Half artery, half artemis,
valve of vibrancy,
how you pump me onward.
Let the world grow silent.

I am listening.

—Joy Sullivan

Table of Contents

Prologue   xiii

1. Earning My Shorts (Trust Your Gut)   1
2. Party of One (Shed Your Shoulds)   21
3. Remaking My Bed (Prioritize. Evolve. Repeat.)   45
4. Grapefruit on the Toilet (Ask For What You Need)   67
5. Front Porch Wieners (Give Yourself a Break)   93
6. Why Me?! (Get Out of Your Own Way)   115
7. Peaches, Please (Embrace the Now)   135
8. F*@$ the Rules (Always Take the Next Best Step)   157

Acknowledgments   177
Author the Author   179
A Gift for You   181

This is a true story about my life—or at least the way I remember it. I've changed a few names and identifying details but, honestly, not many. I hope the folks inside these pages—including those no longer in my life—know how profoundly grateful I am that you have been a part of my story. I wouldn't trade a single season of it for anything.

Prologue

Women are doing it all—running companies, nurturing marriages, raising kids, volunteering on boards, and still making Pinterest-perfect cupcakes for the class party, thank you very much.

But we're exhausted.

We're running on hamster wheels and popping Xanax, and in our most private moments, we're asking ourselves the scariest question of all: *is this it?*

I've been that woman. The harried workaholic. The unhappy wife. The frustrated mom. I was even in a passionate relationship with a woman for two years before marrying my husband. Life's complicated, friends.

The point is I found my way off of the treadmill. And this book is me extending my hand to help you off of yours.

I don't know it all. But I do know this: You are not alone. You are worthy. You are powerful. And you can own your life in such a way that you'll stop asking, *Is this it?* and start saying, *This is it.*

I'm proof.

I've worked in international sales, marketed Fortune 500 brands, and helped launch one of Paul Newman's nonprofit camps for kids.

During some parts, I thrived. During other parts, I merely endured (often while simultaneously "thriving" by societal standards). From all of it, I learned.

I now have the privilege of making a living by coaching women worldwide—from Nike to Wall Street and beyond. Some are young professionals looking for purpose. Others are law partners looking for balance. Most are succeeding but searching, often for something they can't quite identify. I listen to them talk about their stresses, their fears, and their guilt. I help them define success and map strategies to get there. I guide them in prioritizing what matters so they can learn to own their lives. I encourage them to shed their shoulds, make their yeses count, and always take the next best step. I laugh with them. I cry with them. I root for them.

I'm not perfect. There are days I fail. Nights I can't get my girls to bed fast enough so that I can have some silence and wine. Weeks that feel like punches to the professional gut. Truth is I don't always love motherhood. I sometimes break up with clients. There are weeks the nanny gets sick, and my husband is out of town, and I have to figure shit out because I'm the CEO of my company and my family, and it's really hard. (All of which you know. Because you're living it, too.)

But I love my life. My work is purpose-driven and joy-filled, and the Sunday Scaries are no longer a thing. My lover and I take amazing getaways and then get to go home together and parent our babies. My babies are almost out of the toddler years (thank God), which I think means I get to stop carrying so much stuff everywhere we go and that they'll eventually do things while not attached to my leg. I nurture friendships that involve trips to wine country and laughing till we pee. I am not only happy, but I am also content.

This is a story about how I learned to let my heart be boss. And hopefully, it's a story about how you can get there, too.

CHAPTER ONE

Earning My Shorts
{Trust Your Gut}

"I got my own back."

—Maya Angelou

I t was a perfectly stunning fall Friday, with red-orange leaves decorating the city and air so crisp you inhale on purpose. But I was, quite literally, in a dark place—stuck in a windowless conference room on a four-hour call.

Misery.

I knew this job wasn't right. My gut had told me as much during the interview. But it was a sexy position at a nationally respected marketing agency, working with high-profile clients. Plus, it was 2009, in the heart of the recession. Opportunities like this were rare.

I started the gig on a Monday. By Wednesday, I felt physically ill. On Thursday, I called my friend Miguel, who had witnessed my transformation over the past few years as I had carefully and intentionally evolved into exactly who I wanted to be.

"I can't stand this fucking job," I said.

"You've put in too much work to stop now," he replied.

Now, I knew, was not the time to lead with my head. It was time to let my heart be boss. But could I?

By Friday, I was stuck in that windowless conference room on a call that might never actually end.

No worries, I tried to tell myself. *Suck it up. Power through.*

It's what I always did. I am a rule-follower, an over-deliverer, an above-and-beyonder. But all those little things I did to make everyone else happy while ignoring what my own gut was telling me—all those *shoulds*—were exactly how I ended up in the unhappy marriage and unhappy life I was finally emerging from. Now here I was, four and a quarter days into a dream job, knowing wholeheartedly that it was someone else's dream. If I survived the week, I feared that the golden handcuffs would be locked too tightly for me ever to conjure up the nerve to leave.

My brain stayed calm: *Power through. Power through. Power through.* My gut threw a tantrum of proportions so epic I could have puked.

A quick intermission—yes, the call was that long—gave me the chance to turn to my manager.

"I'm sorry," I said. "This just isn't for me."

It was perhaps the first time in my professional life that instead of doing what I *should* do, I did what I was *called* to do.

I didn't know it then, of course, but the move would earn me one hell of a party story and a nickname I proudly carry to this day: One-Week Walsh. It would mean that, since I lacked a trust fund and a life partner, I would become a thirty-year-old, shorts-wearing, warehouse-organizing, paper-pushing intern for my family's heating and cooling company as I looked for my next gig. But it would also allow me to rewrite my story.

So while my (former) team and their client dove back onto that call, I gathered my things, grabbed my bag, went outside, and drank some air. As I walked toward my condo, I passed a park. A man dressed as a clown—makeup and all—rode past me on a unicycle, gleeful. I laughed out loud.

What a beautiful sign, I thought. Pursue joy. Whatever that looks like for you. If this guy could do it, I damn well could, too.

I hadn't a clue what lay ahead. But on that brilliant, beautiful day, I chose to step away from the dream I should have wanted and toward the joy I craved.

I was unemployed and blissful.

One of These Things Is Not Like the Others

I wasn't good at school. Not naturally, at least.

I'm a lefty, so I was often out of place, awkward at using scissors and opening cans, bumping elbows in tight spaces, writing "wrong." I'm the youngest of six, many of whom are not just book smart but book brilliant, so I felt slow and lesser. I also processed information differently than everyone else. I reasoned differently. And different isn't necessarily celebrated.

But my emotional intelligence was through the roof. Of course, I didn't know what it was called or, at least as a kid, that it was an asset. But I understood people. And feelings. I liked when people were happy, hated when people were sad, and could usually figure out how to bridge that gap. I learned how to make people feel comfortable. How to ask good questions. How to listen intently.

Beyond natural empathy, I also had the gift of strong intuition. I never fully understood algebra. And I didn't score high enough on the ACT to get into the same university where all five of my siblings earned their degrees. (I discovered years later that my sweet father even wrote them a note pleading my case to no avail.) But I've always had a sixth sense—and a damn strong sense of self.

My dad was an entrepreneur and devout Catholic who cared about community, friendships, and doing the right thing. Despite being an active father of six, for example, he was also a Big Brother to a kid who didn't have a dad in his life. Ours was the house where everyone was welcome (and when you multiply the welcoming by two outgoing parents and six kids, we were basically a community hall). And Dad hated—I mean *hated*—pretense. He and Mom lived below their means and didn't give a shit about keeping up with the Joneses. I worshipped Dad, so I didn't either.

But by the end of my senior year of college, as friends started securing jobs, my confidence—inwardly, at least—started to falter. One evening, as I walked up the front path to the sorority house, a group of friends who all had received not only job offers but also signing bonuses were walking out.

"What are you up to?" I asked.

"We're going out to dinner to celebrate that we have jobs," one said and kept on moving.

I walked up the stairs to my room and cried. It sucked.

Around the same time, my college leadership group took a trip to New York to talk with alumni. One of them threw us a cocktail party with his high-powered friends. I stood in his swanky Chelsea apartment wearing black pants, black booties, and a gray button-up shirt from Italy that I had brought home from my semester abroad. I felt good. Suddenly, Silicon Alley pioneer Cella Irvine—holder of degrees from Cornell and Harvard, who would eventually lead About.com—powered into the room, all strength and sophistication. A woman in tech in the '90s? Yes, please. I watched her grab a flute of champagne and work the room before she made her way to our group.

"What are you doing after graduation?" she asked.

Several of my peers rattled off their signing-bonus jobs. It was a moment that could have tempted anyone to be fake. Maybe it was liquid courage that kicked in. Or perhaps it was Dad, not giving a shit about the Joneses. But I didn't spin anything.

"Maybe travel? I don't know," I said. Then, as everyone looked at me blankly, bubbles fizzing in their flutes, horrified at my response, I started singing the words to a song from a childhood TV show about one of these things being unlike the others.

Cella roared.

"You *shouldn't* know!" she said.

Four months later, one of my signing-bonus friends had already been laid off, I was flying first-class to Amsterdam for my job, and Cella was well on her way to becoming a lifelong mentor of mine.

One of these things is not like the others. She is, she hopes, like her dad.

IS THIS IT?
FOLLOWING YOUR GUT TO FIND YOUR HAPPY

Is this it?

We've all asked it at some point, haven't we? It's a question so scary we don't want to admit we've considered it. Still, there it can sit, in those quiet moments so many of us overfill our lives to avoid.

My clients—mostly women in their thirties, forties, and fifties who outwardly seem to be thriving in their lives—ask it a lot. They're on that hamster wheel, running feverishly. Career. Partner. Kids. Community. Friends. Faith. Soccer tournament. Birthday party. School party. Shit—I'm on cupcake duty. Mom will watch the kids. Early flight. Presentation. Have I cooked a meal for my family this month?

It's fucking exhausting.

You already know that, though. But what's scarier than the exhaustion is asking those three little words. Because this is exactly what you've worked your whole life to attain, right? Here you are!

Is this it?

Sometimes, we have no idea why we're asking it. Other times, we know exactly why we're asking; we're just not sure how to change things.

I believe this question stems from two central places: boredom and restriction. We're doing the same job or in the same relationship or (gulp) parenting the same kids, and it loses its luster. Or we feel stuck—unsure where to start or unable to find a way to do what our guts are telling us to do.

Here's where I suggest starting: rediscover your passion.

That passion might be the same as it was when you were a kid, but somehow, it's gotten buried so low on your priority list that you hardly remember what it was. Or that passion might be completely new or different from what it was twenty or ten or even two years ago when you started your career or your company or your family.

Your passion is your fuel. It gives you purpose and power. If you can incorporate it into your everyday life, you'll stop feeling like you're living for everyone else and losing yourself in the process.

With my clients, I have found the Perfect Day exercise very effective, so I'll invite you to try it.

How do you really want to feel? Think about it.

Now, write down what it would take in one day to feel that way. What is the environment? When do you wake up? Who are you interacting with? What are you doing? Be romantic. Have no limits.

Then, explore that day. Which themes currently exist? Which don't? What's realistic? How can we get there—and sustain that?

Finally, this: what is one step you can take today to get closer?

This—whatever this is for you—doesn't have to be it. Your gut has the answers. Let it be your guide to happy.

Dad

My dad would always go trick-or-treating with my friends and me when we were kids. Inevitably, every year, he'd walk ahead a few houses, and we'd get lost in who got what and anticipate what treats were coming next. Then, all of a sudden, he'd leap out of a pile of leaves in the neighbor's yard, which, 100 percent of the time, caused my best friend to pee her pants.

Leo Walsh was super fun.

He was the dad who got home from work, took off his tie, and played. He'd shoot the basketball with me or pitch me balls.

Some evenings, we'd get on our bikes and ride to Helen Hutchley's, our local ice cream shop. It was probably two miles away, but it felt like a giant deal to ride that far. The trip required navigating three hills and one very busy road—an adventure, for sure. (I always preferred the tandem for obvious reasons. I'm guessing Dad did not.) He always ordered butter pecan and ate it in a minute. He taught most of the kids in the neighborhood how to ride a bike, too. And he'd line us up to practice before the annual civic association's Labor Day bike race, stopwatch in hand.

Dad always wanted to put me in situations that would allow for the most growth, even if it made me feel uncomfortable. So, when it came time for basketball in sixth grade, he signed me up for the boys' league.

When my high school sweetheart, whom I had written to daily after he joined the military, called things off, I was devastated. Dad sat out on the back patio and talked with me about life and love.

You know how in college some people gain the Freshman Fifteen? Thanks to a steady diet of Papa John's breadsticks and Diet Coke, mine became the Junior Thirty. I hated feeling chubby, and I said so. One day, Dad sent me a can of SlimFast and fresh carrots.

The carrots were still cold, like they had just been selected from the produce section. He wasn't trying to be rude; he just wanted to help. My friend Jamie and I laugh about that still. How were those carrots still cold?

Mail from Dad, in fact, was the norm—even for my friends. He'd often attach articles from the *Wall Street Journal* and encourage me to get into politics. "There need to be more women in Washington!" he wrote in a letter I still have. "Run for office!" He sometimes sent money. And when he did, he always instructed me to use it for my highest priority—like, "Use this for books or to go canoeing, whichever is higher on your priority list." He was my first and best life coach.

Dad worked hard in an industry I didn't see as glamorous to provide for our family and give his children opportunities he never had. I remember calling him from the train station in Luxembourg while I studied abroad. I had just spent a week in Italy and was telling him about Vatican City.

"I've never been to Rome," he said. "I'll look forward to seeing the Vatican one day."

He wasn't paying me lip service. Dad loved God, he loved Catholicism, and he would, I knew, love the Vatican. I couldn't wait for him to see it for himself. For Christmas, Mom gave Dad a stack of books about traveling to Italy. They planned a trip for the summer of 2001.

By the time we rang in that new year, I was fresh out of college and living in New York—well, Hoboken, New Jersey, actually, where rent was still astronomical, but at least I had more than fifteen square feet of space. I was twenty-two, working under a nurturing boss, helping to execute corporate events around the world, making good money, and globetrotting on the company's dime. Jackpot.

Our team spent the first week of the year in ritzy Dubai. By January 19, we were on a plane to San Diego.

We landed late at night, checked into our room, and almost immediately went to bed. When I woke up in the morning, I had over a dozen missed calls from my siblings. I looked at my boss, Colleen.

"I'm scared," I said. I could feel it in my soul. "I know one of my parents is dead."

Colleen sat on her bed, quiet and still, as I carried my phone onto the small balcony. I called my parents' house and two siblings before finally getting through to a third.

Mike was crying when he picked up.

"Dad died," he said.

Colleen packed my bag, booked me a first-class ticket home, took me to the airport, and sat with me until I boarded the plane.

I landed in Columbus a few minutes before my brothers Mike and Pat arrived from Chicago.

"Regan, I'm so sorry," Pat kept repeating through sobs that echoed throughout baggage claim. "I'm so sorry."

All of my siblings recognized that I had been robbed—the youngest of the pack who got the fewest years with Dad. We sat in the TV room at Mom and Dad's house and wrote the obituary together. We tried finding solace in the fact that he had died just as he once told my mother he wanted to—playing handball. He had played his usual Saturday morning game with an old friend. After they wrapped, he had a heart attack that killed him instantly. No drawn-out illness. No suffering.

His work on earth was, apparently, complete.

The two-day celebration of his life was epic. The wake was first. Hundreds of people stood in line to pay their respects. Dad's lifetime barber combed his hair in the casket. Dad wore a handsome shirt with cufflinks I had given him for Christmas a few weeks earlier.

The funeral was the following day—appropriately, the coldest day of the year. I remember all of us standing with Mom, preparing to walk into the room with the casket before they closed it.

This year, instead of celebrating her fortieth anniversary with Dad, Mom was burying him. But she didn't wilt. She found strength for us.

"OK," Mom said. "Now, we're going to say goodbye to Daddy."

After the funeral, we hosted a big party, fireworks included, at our house. Two of my New York friends flew in for the event. One had generously brought me a bag of clothes because I had left Hoboken with a suitcase full of warm-weather outfits suitable for San Diego's sunshine and palm trees, not burying my dad in an Ohio winter. The other walked around each room with a trash bag, picking up used plates, cups, and forks—just getting shit done. There are friends, and then there are friends. These were the latter, and I was grateful.

Now, as an adult, most of the people in my life never knew my father. I have come to cherish those who did. Once, at a fundraising event, I met someone in Dad's industry and asked if he was familiar with Dad's company. "Leo Walsh is your dad?!" he said. "You look just like him!" Another time, after speaking at an event, four older men approached me. "We knew your dad," one said. "He was always such a great business owner. He really provided value, and he helped us a lot." And on a girls' trip to Napa Valley, we met a man at a vineyard from Naperville, near Chicago. "My dad grew up there," I said. His mom did, too. I called my husband and had him dig up Dad's yearbook; our parents were classmates. I have to believe that those instances are never accidents but gifts of connection from a higher power. Little reminders of big love. I relish them.

During my senior year in college, for Dads' Weekend at Ohio University, Dad had driven the hour and a half down to campus after work. He wasn't the dad who would stay a whole weekend; he was sixty-four and not about to be up all night at a gross hole-in-the-wall drinking quarter drafts. But he wanted to show up for me and take me to dinner. I took him to Zachary's, the fanciest bar in town, so he could get a proper Rob Roy and a good New York-style deli sandwich. We walked back to my sorority house after we ate.

"Regan," he said, "I'm sorry I'm not younger like all the other dads. Your mother and I parented you and Michael very differently. Not better or worse than your siblings, just different."

He drove off, and I cried.

I never had the guts to tell him that I didn't care that he was older because he was still cool. And he was wise. And he and my mom had a healthier relationship than any of my friends' parents.

I am so honored to be his daughter.

THE TALKING GUT

A client recently sent me a note.

"My gut is starting to speak loudly to me."

"Starting?" I asked. "No, it always has. You're just listening now."

Perhaps you've tuned yours out, too, because you didn't like what it was telling you. (Don't apply for that job—it's power, yes, but the stress will make you miserable. Stop taking on so many clients—the money isn't worth your sanity.) Or maybe you're simply unfamiliar with how your gut communicates.

Our gut speaks to us in moments of positivity and negativity. It tells you when something's a no and something's a go. Here are a few ways your gut might be trying to communicate something to you.

Negative: you feel instant dread.

When we make decisions without thought or intention, we often experience instant regret—that nagging feeling of foreboding. We ask ourselves, *Why did I agree to this?* And we do that because we didn't ask the question before we made the commitment. Dread is a gut reaction, a quick and easy way to recognize that we've made the wrong decision and should perhaps shift gears.

Positive: you feel laser-focused.

Often, when something is jiving with your gut, it's almost hard to stop thinking about it. Your next steps are in clear focus, and you show up for yourself like never before, tackling tasks and achieving goals with a concentration most would envy. It's not that it's easy—it's just that your gut knows it's worth it.

Negative: you have physical pain.

I talk about this a lot with clients. Our gut often takes desperate measures to get our attention, manifesting as bodily pain to let us know something isn't quite right. I've had a lot of clients who hate their nine-to-five jobs tell me they feel physically sick on Sundays or during their morning drive. In a past life, when I was regularly tuning out my gut, I found myself with acute shoulder tension. Take note of these pains, and try to draw connections.

Positive: it's easy to be silly.

Ever make a big decision and then find yourself feeling almost silly with joy? That's how I felt when I once quit a demanding job. In the weeks leading up to my last day, I'd blast Beyoncé (who else?) and dance in my bathroom. I was exceptionally joyful, and that made it easy to be silly. Silliness could be your gut's way of celebrating, too.

When it comes to how we use our expendable resources—time and energy—our gut is always talking.

Antennas up, ladies.

Earning My Shorts

Months later, I was still reeling from Dad's death when the planes crashed into the towers on 9/11. It took a sledgehammer to a heart trying desperately to heal.

Soon, my company, like many others, buckled under the fallout.

And by October, like many others, I had been laid off.

I searched for jobs that didn't seem to exist. After a rough few months, pharmaceutical giant Eli Lilly offered me a position in sales. It wasn't my best and highest calling, but with my rent running high and my severance pay running low, it was the lifeboat I needed. I was grateful.

Still, life felt dark. Dad was dead. The world was on edge. Jobs were scarce—let alone jobs you felt passionate about. I was shaken. I no longer felt like the small-town girl who could conquer the big city. I felt like the small-town girl overwhelmed by life.

So I wasn't exactly me when I met Mark. Regardless, he liked me.

Mark felt familiar—an Ohio boy who, like me, grew up in a big, Irish Catholic family where parties are chaotic and children are everywhere. He worked in IT and was every bit the patient problem-solver you would expect. He could read a map.[1] And he was kind. He brought me quarters for the Laundromat. And once, on an especially cold night, he drove his car to my neighborhood, found a parking spot close to my apartment, and waited there until I arrived home so I could take it.

He didn't light me up or make me laugh. He preferred staying in to going out. He wasn't the man of my dreams. He probably wasn't even a decent fit for me, or I for him. My mother noted as much, as gently and respectfully as she could have.

---

1 My dad could read a map. So can all six of his kids. I once had a date who used a Garmin to get me two miles from dinner to my condo, which was two turns away. I knew the moment he cued that thing up that there wouldn't be a date number two. I could pretend it's about navigating more than streets. But really, it's not. If you can't get two fucking miles without electronic help, I cannot sleep with you. Next.

But on July 4 (see, he knew my favorite day, and that's something, right?), this good and decent young man took me on a walk near my mother's house. As he got down on one knee to ask me for forever, he trembled. My stomach churned.

No, no, no, no, no. My gut couldn't have been more decisive.

"Yes," I said.

Our marriage was fine. We went through the motions, smiled through dinner, occasionally had ho-hum sex, and eventually transferred back to Columbus, Ohio, to be close to our families. Soon, fine turned to absolute boredom. And boredom turned into apathy. We didn't fight—there wasn't enough passion for that. We barely even talked. I was living in a haze.

Is this it?

But I was a good Catholic girl, and good Catholic girls should stay. So I did.

Eventually, my boss and friend Miguel encouraged me to try a beginner's series he was teaching in Muay Thai, the sport of Thai boxing. My first class was a flurry of jumping jacks, high knees, jump squats, and kicks that bruised my feet. I thought I might vomit, but I was hooked. I started fantasizing about drop-kicking coworkers I couldn't stand.

The people at the gym were weird and wonderful. Gay. Straight. Students. Parents. Entrepreneurs. I didn't realize how badly I was craving community until suddenly I had one.

My family feared it was a cult. Mark was wary, too. But for the first time since Dad died, I was happy. Happy enough in one aspect of life to realize how utterly unhappy I was in another. I finally asked

Mark to see a therapist. We went to one session together. Then we both went separately.

"If I put a gun to your head, and you have to stay in this marriage or go, what do you do?" the therapist asked.

Go! my gut screamed.

"Go," I said.

"I can't help you, then," the therapist replied.

My appointment ended almost as soon as it began.

Around that same time, I was testing for my first Muay Thai shorts, which is a process similar to earning a martial arts belt. Mark's family was in town to cheer on his sister as she ran the Columbus Marathon. They went to watch Ohio State's football team play Notre Dame, where many of them had gone to school, while I went to the gym.

It was among the greatest nights of my life.

As about a hundred people watched, a dozen of us lined up horizontally to show our technical skills. With a partner holding pads in front of us, we demonstrated the basics in unison—front kicks, roundhouse kicks, jabs, crosses.

Then, we moved on to the individual round. Here's how it goes: each student has six minutes to showcase his or her skills in what amounts to a mock fight. For the first five minutes, a senior student holds pads that you punch and kick. For the final minute, the gym's owner—Amal, a human lightning bolt of grit and energy and muscle, and maybe the most intimidating person I ever had met—holds a shield to combat your advances. You must impress her.

I went first.

The hundred people formed a circle around me and my friend Miguel, who stood before me holding the pads. I wanted to set the tone.

Do not hold back.

The timer started, and the first three minutes felt like thirty. I was soaked with sweat.

Jab. Cross. Jab. Cross. Front kick. Jab. Roundhouse. Cross.

People screamed, clapped, cheered. I fed on it.

Front kick, jab, jab, jab, cross.

Amal emerged with her shield. The cheers grew louder. I wanted to collapse. Instead, I found another level.

Jab, cross, jab, cross, roundhouse, jab, jab, jab, front kick.

Buzzzzzzz.

The timer sounded, and the group descended in, shouting and hugging my soaked, depleted body. I experienced a new level of emotion. Elation, perhaps? My highest high, for sure.

Dad, I knew, would have been proud.

Throughout the night, I coughed up blood, but I didn't care.

I earned my shorts.

And at the same time, I finally conjured up the courage to walk to the edge of the cliff I had long been avoiding.

I waited, of course, until Mark's family was gone. Then we sat down together at our small kitchen table.

"I don't want to be married," I said.

"How long have you been feeling this way?" he asked.

I explained that it had been a long time coming. That I had given it my best go. That it wasn't fair for either of us.

He didn't yell. Didn't cry. Didn't fight.

"OK," he said simply.

He stood up, packed one bag, and left.

We only talked one other time before filing our papers.

I've spent so much time and had so many talks with friends trying to unpack that chapter. Thing is, at the end of the day, it's as simple and as human as this: I made a mistake.

I should have listened to my gut on our first date, and on our second, and on our third. I should have listened to it when Mark was on his knee shaking.

The good news is, even after we ignore them, our guts never stop talking.

Our only job is to listen—and act.

If you can't see the sunlight from the conference room, friends, stand up, gather your stuff, and get the hell out.

CHAPTER TWO

Party of One
{Shed Your Shoulds}

"To thine own self be true."
—William Shakespeare

The party was being hosted at the home of a high-profile executive of a Fortune 500 company. Only it wasn't being hosted by her. It was being hosted by her teenage daughter, who, unbeknownst to Mom, was throwing a holiday rager. Once we had raged to our heart's content, three of us left and got into Annie's Bronco. She was sober. Her boyfriend and I, not so much.

We started to cruise our pretty little suburb, where Christmas decorations lit up perfectly manicured lawns. When Annie's boyfriend needed to pee, we pulled over. He returned to the Bronco holding a Santa Claus. Hilarious! Thus began our quest. We stopped at a couple dozen houses, snagging lawn ornaments along the way, drunk on cheap beer, laughing until we cried. We popped into my house so I could call my crush.

"We're on our way. Meet us outside," I said. "Don't ask questions."

He crawled into the Bronco—so crowded with plastic reindeer and snowmen that Annie had pulled a Santa onto her lap to make room for him—and laughed. Within minutes, though, we heard the sirens behind us. Busted.

We had to go to Saturday school and do community service. On top of our official punishment, Annie and I felt so much shame we went door to door apologizing for our behavior. And I really meant those sorrys. I hated disappointing people. I hated disappointing myself.

That, friends, is the only time I've ever been in trouble.

I was Miss Arlington—the one-time reigning queen of our sweet little bubble of a city, which is situated alongside Ohio State University and home to all sorts of famous athletes and business professionals. I was secretary of the student council in high school, where I earned favor among teachers with a friendly demeanor and fierce work ethic. And in college, I became president of my sorority. As a sophomore. I wasn't a goody-goody. (I mean, I'm Irish Catholic, and as a general rule, we like booze.) But underage drinking aside, I followed the rules. I made people happy. I over-delivered. I wanted you to be proud of me. It didn't even matter whether you knew me. That's how obedient I was.

In middle school, when my friends decided to sneak out at a sleepover to meet another group at the park, I felt physically ill. We hid in the ditch when cars drove by. I don't even know what we did when we got to the park. I hated every second.

And in college, when I studied abroad in Luxembourg, I traveled

one weekend to Italy. My brother, his wife, and their infant baby—
who I hadn't yet met—were there for a month-long sabbatical. They
invited me to take the train a few hours south and spend a couple of days with them. To admire art. To eat pizza. To play with
that precious babe. But instead of extending my trip to visit them,
I returned to Luxembourg so as not to miss a class. And my study
abroad classes were pass/fail. That's the kind of sometimes-regretful
rule-follower I always was.

I did what I should.

Doing what you should is, in some cases, good—and in other
cases, great. It makes you a likable kid. A likable friend. A likable
student. A likable employee. People who do what they should are
dependable. I love being that. You can count on me!

Problem is doing what you should is, in other cases, bad. Namely
for you. And its ripple effect can wreak havoc on everyone around
you. At some point, you see, I became so programmed to do what I
should that I stopped asking what I wanted.

It's where a lot of us unwittingly end up—in a space where we
should our lives away. We *should* keep that job and all the security
that comes with it, even if it's making us crazy. We *should* keep that
husband and all the order that comes with him, even if he's making
us miserable. We *should* serve on that board. Lead that Girl Scout
troop. Attend that fundraiser. The list goes on.

When I worked at Eli Lilly, I was miserable. I was always tense
and suffered severe shoulder pain. I daydreamed of hitting the lot-
tery (on a particularly terrible day, I even went and bought a ticket)
or opening a bakery (I definitely tried convincing my friend Kelly

to audition for a Food Network reality baking show). But I was making a good salary, with good benefits and good stock options. I *should* keep this job. Suck it up. Power on. And for years, I did. It never occurred to me I had choices.

When I was a bright-eyed, fresh-out-of-college Midwestern girl living in Hoboken, I knew exactly what New Year's Eve in New York should look like. And so I planned it. My besties came into town. We all bought hundred-dollar tickets to a warehouse club in SoHo where live bands played throughout the night. I met a cute investment banker there who graduated from Yale and was super psyched to tell me about it. At one point, as my friends and I hopped between floors on the stairwell, splashes of liquid sprayed on us. *What is that?* we wondered. And then Tara looked up, where a man was on the top floor with his penis out. "It's pee!" Tara screamed. Nothing says New Year's in New York like a stranger's urine on your killer outfit, eh?

A few years later—the year I finally called off my marriage—I spent New Year's Eve alone in my house. I popped open a bottle of champagne, turned on Snoop Dogg, and danced so hard I was sweating. It wasn't how anyone *should* spend New Year's. It was, instead, perfect.

So weeks after Mark had moved out, at the end of a fantastic party with my Muay Thai friends, when I found myself sitting alone on a couch with that lightning bolt of a woman who owned the gym, I didn't do what I should have. Instead, I kissed her back. It kicked off a chapter nobody would have expected—me included. But I don't have a single regret.

All of it led me to the man I would marry, the daughters I adore, the career I relish, and the ability to thrive. Shedding my shoulds has allowed me to open my mind, make my yeses count, and ultimately experience life in a completely new way.

JUST SAY NO:
A GUIDE TO SHEDDING YOUR SHOULDS

We're yessing ourselves to death—or at least into anxiety-ridden existences.

With clients, I witness a whole lot of hemming, hawing, and ultimately regret when it comes to our inability to just say no. Because the hard truth is this: we have limited resources. Saying yes to any and every half-decent opportunity that comes our way leaves us overcommitted, spread thin, and burned out. We end up disappointing ourselves and the people who matter most.

I once coached an executive in the insurance industry who, outside of her nine-to-five, was on four different boards and in a handful of industry-specific associations. She was quite literally running herself ragged, being pulled in a million different directions and feeling physically ill at the idea of attending so many meetings. All because she thought she *should*.

Should is a dangerous place to live. It weighs us down and causes us to overcommit and underperform. (That goes for you too, companies.) We gather data from our friends, family, and society and make decisions based on the perception we want to project to them. But oftentimes, we just end up with shoulds.

When I talk with clients about this topic, I like to focus on that sense of inner knowing. What is your body telling you about this particular opportunity, this particular should? Do you feel drained? Frustrated? If you're a company, are your employees feeling this way? Then it's probably worth shedding.

We need to learn to discriminate against anything that distracts us from our growth and goals. Our time is limited, so why waste it on something that doesn't have meaning? Why dilute our yeses by giving out too many?

The thing is we know that. So why do we avoid no like the plague?

First and foremost: we avoid it out of fear. We're afraid we'll miss out on new business if we turn down that coffee meeting, or we're afraid we'll disappoint our kid's teacher if we say no to bringing snacks.

Often, we say yes to something so we can be seen a certain way—reliable, connected, overachieving. *What will people think of me?* we wonder, even subconsciously. Meanwhile, we ignore our own needs and priorities, and then we just feel crummy.

I also think we fall into the yes trap when we believe we need an excuse to say no. I once went to a concert with a client because I felt I didn't have a good enough excuse not to. I'm an in-bed-by-nine gal, and I'm certainly not a fan of crowds. But there I was on a Thursday night, standing in a mosh pit listening to a band I was clearly only pretending to enjoy. (Note: if you have to fake something—anything—why are you saying yes?)

I'm here to help with three potentially life-changing questions to help you just say no. Ask yourself these questions before ever letting a yes or no out, and you'll set yourself up for happy.

Does This Align With My Core Values?

Walking away from appealing offers becomes a whole lot easier when we have clarity of purpose, which means we understand and honor our priorities by saying yes only to those things that align with our values.

What are yours? Consider the eight areas that make up the life wheel: family, work, money, personal growth, health and wellness, spirituality, community, and living environment. Pick three, and commit to them, giving yourself permission to say no to the opportunities that fall outside of those three buckets.

This, of course, is nuanced. In this season of my life, I am putting personal growth, work, and family first. Consequently, I turn down quite a few pro bono speaking opportunities (despite the fact that they benefit organizations I support) because they interfere with time I'd like to spend growing myself, growing my business, or nurturing the people I love most. Instead of giving my time, I give financially to the causes that inspire me. I make the occasional exception when it makes sense for my work, or simply because it's compelling, but not without considerable thought.

Know your core values—and let them guide you.

If I Say Yes to This, What Am I Saying No To?

When values compete, saying no gets a whole lot harder. So we have to be vigilant about pinpointing what we're giving up when we say yes to something—and what we're gaining by saying no.

Despite my familiarity with this truth, I admittedly still struggle with it. I recently made an exception to my no-pro-bono rule. I agreed to a speaking engagement because the cause inspired me, and I knew I could make some meaningful connections at the event. But as the day approached, I found myself feeling more and more dread. I hadn't stopped long enough to think about what I'd be giving up: precious weekend time with my family.

When you're considering something, take a moment to ask yourself what's at stake. What are you subconsciously telling yourself and those around you when you begrudgingly say yes? (You don't value your own time or needs.) How will you feel about what you've given up in exchange? (Frustrated, depleted, etc.)

As emails flood your inbox at the end of the day, and you feel compelled to stick around and reply, pause and consider the cost. If that means missing dinner at home, something you've done before and regretted, perhaps the emails can wait.

How Much Do I *Actually* Want To Do This?
We can also more easily avoid regret if we take the time to consider how genuine our desire for something is. This takes us back to the shoulds—those things we do because we think we *should*, not because we've actually stopped to consider our true feelings.

One of the simplest ways to measure our true desires is to follow Greg McKeown's 90 percent rule. In his book *Essentialism*, McKeown suggests ranking opportunities on a scale from one to one hundred. If the invite or request ranks below a ninety, move it to a zero and politely decline. "If something is just or almost good enough," he writes, "then the answer should be a no." This allows you to filter out your watered-down yeses so you have a clear purpose behind each decision.

And I'm here to tell you that this pays off. I once turned down an invite I'd ranked an eighty-seven. It was appealing, but it teetered on the edge of being something I really wanted to do. A few weeks later, a total one hundred came along. Had I said yes to that eighty-seven, I would've had to turn down the one hundred. It solidified my belief in this rule.

Saying no to the eighty-sevens, sixty-fives, and twenty-threes leaves room for the opportunities that significantly impact our lives, and the lives of those around us, in positive ways.

As you become more liberal with your noes, don't be afraid of speaking your truth. Because ultimately, if you can't say no, your yes doesn't mean anything.

Run toward what makes you happy.

Chrysalis

As I drove slowly through the snow to pick up Carrie for our first Muay Thai class, I felt nervous. Our friend Miguel was in charge of the beginner's program, and he asked us to sign up. So we did. But now, it was the dead of winter in Ohio. Carrie's car was actually lodged in the snow, which is why I was rolling up to her place. And the idea of peeling off layers of clothes to bust my ass trying a new martial art felt less than ideal. Also, I didn't want to suck at it.

We walked through the dark toward the concrete block of a gym, opened the door, and *bam*. Bright lights shined on blue mats covering the floor. A fighting ring stood in the corner. Music blared. The sounds of punches and kicks echoed.

The people were different. Different ages. Different genders. Different colors. Different sexual orientations.

It felt like an alternate universe from the one I lived a few miles away, where the man I was unhappily married to was sitting in our quiet living room alone, tapping his laptop. Where I would have been sitting silently across the room from him if I was there, mindlessly watching TV.

Class was hell. Wiping the sweat. Fighting the puke. Relishing the energy. My feet would be bruised from the kicking by morning, but I didn't care.

I was hooked.

This buzz—it made me feel alive. It made everyone feel alive. So it's easy to understand, then, why people worshipped Amal, the mastermind behind the gym.

Amal—or, as leaders in Muay Thai are known, our Kru—was a petite powerhouse of solid muscle, with a beautiful mane of thick black hair and dark, serious eyes. I was terrified of her at first. Everyone was. We wanted to please her. To be the recipients of that chiseled face softening into her wide smile.

Where Amal went, we followed. To grab beers after class. To watch her play with her band in a little downtown bar. "It's weird," my brother said, "the way you all follow each other around. The way you only want to be together."

What they didn't know (because I didn't tell them) was how despondent I was at home. How bored. How unfulfilled.

Muay Thai became my lifeline. It brought me joy. Taught me just how strong I am. And after a year, ultimately gave me the courage to leave my husband.

A month after Mark moved out, I was feeling a jumble of

emotions—confusion, excitement, guilt—when I walked up to Amal's apartment for a Halloween dinner party with gym friends.

"Hey!" Amal opened the door dressed as a prisoner in an orange jumpsuit and shackles.

I had showed up sans costume. I hate the pressure of dressing up. Plus, I had no intention of going to another house party with the group afterward. So I stood there in a cute black dress and black boots.

"What are you?" someone asked.

"I," I joked, "am going to be her conjugal visit."

The group howled.

We devoured Indian food, drank cocktails, laughed. As the others eventually filtered out, Amal and I stayed on her couch, deep in conversation. She had just ended a five-year relationship. We lamented our breakups. She talked about her recent trip to see the Dalai Lama. We got raging drunk. On cocktails. On life. On each other.

And suddenly, nobody was talking, and she was leaning in, and I couldn't help but kiss her back. It was warm. And wonderful. And exciting. And electric. And holy shit, what is happening? And why the hell does it feel so damn good?

It was a one-time thing. Obviously. I shouldn't have done it. I'm straight. She's the Kru.

I showed up for class on Monday shy and embarrassed. Amal laughed. I laughed. It was fine. Thank God.

Later that week, I called Amal to walk me through making a Manhattan over the phone. We both talked nervously. Like we wanted to see each other again. But she wasn't going to initiate the invite, and I was too nervous to know what to do. As she told me what ingredients to gather, I combed my kitchen. I was missing vermouth.

"Just come over here," she said. "I'll make you one."

Hallelujah. Shit.

Our chemistry was crazy. Magnetic. I just did what felt good. And it all felt good. "You'll never have better sex," Amal said. I wondered if she was right.

One night, when we all went to the bar to watch Amal's band, she introduced a new song, "Come Home With Me." She looked at me as she sang. Was I blushing? Did people know? What am I doing?

Amal was sensitive and perceptive and considerate, with strong intuition like mine. A great listener. A badass with depth in her soul. She is the first person I really opened up to about struggling in school. I told her how I always felt stupid, and she held me as I cried. I cried a lot about my dad to her. I once told her Dad bought us a certain kind of socks every year for Christmas. That Christmas, she gifted me those socks. I confided my physical insecurities, and she told me I was beautiful. I wore a bikini for the first time in my life on vacation with her.

Back home, we would lay in the hammock together and talk. Cook dinners. Drink Manhattans. Walk in the park. The trees were extra green, the sky was extra blue, everything was extra beautiful.

But as time wore on, we fought a lot, too. Amal loved having people around, and I relish being alone. So I was in a wildly anxious season—getting divorced—with an exotic woman who needed to be connected all the time. One morning, she offered to make me coffee. I just wanted space to get breakfast and coffee to go from my favorite café and get to the office early.

"I don't have time," I said.

So I left her place and went to the restaurant—where, because she wasn't cooking for me, Amal happened to show up.

"I thought you didn't have time for breakfast," she said, equal parts hurt and angry.

She was almost forty, and she was ready to settle down. To start her forever. To have kids. I, meanwhile, had only told a few select friends I was even dating a woman. One of my brothers heard a rumor about us. I stumbled through an explanation when he called. Amal felt wounded that I wasn't shouting about our relationship from the rooftops. But I was just living day by day. A caterpillar tucked into a chrysalis. Becoming whoever I was supposed to become.

Round and round we would go. Argue, break up, make up. Argue, break up, make up.

There was so much love, but so much pain, too. At one point, it simply had to stop.

As difficult as it was—and it was really, really difficult—I eventually chose to leave the gym. It was too much for me, and it was unfair to her.

But that woman and that gym are among my most important chapters. They brought me back to life. They gave me space to grow my wings.

WHAT YOU AREN'T CHANGING, YOU'RE CHOOSING

I can't leave this job. It's secure. The benefits are great. And my stock options might split someday.

I repeated those words to myself for five years. Five. Years. I hated that job. But for all of the reasons listed above, I felt I had to stay, despite my unhappiness. I didn't have a choice. Sound familiar?

What you aren't changing, you're choosing.

My yoga instructor said this one day, and I resisted the urge to give her a standing ovation. It's the thing I repeat to my clients (and myself) all the time.

It's so easy to convince ourselves that we don't have a choice, isn't it? If I've learned anything from coaching (and from my own lived experiences), it's that we're very good at tuning into societal norms, the opinions of others, and fear of the unknown when we make our decisions. We let them tell us what we should do—and you know how I feel about shoulds.

This does two very bad things: It makes us feel trapped in jobs, relationships, and situations that aren't suited for us. And it removes our autonomy, stripping our ability to make decisions using our gut as our guide. After all, our gut often asks us to do scary things—things that make us uncomfortable—and it's easier to tell ourselves, "I have no choice."

But we're always choosing, even when we say we aren't.

Every time we wake up and go to a job we hate, we're choosing. Every time we avoid hard conversations with loved ones, we're choosing. Every time we ignore our intuition and say yes to shoulds, we're choosing.

I didn't fully realize it at the time, but I was choosing to stay in a job I hated. I'm so glad I finally listened to my gut and left.

Years ago, during my NYU coaching training, I attended a poetry reading at a classmate's apartment. The poem, titled "Diving In," struck me. It uses the analogy of leaping into a cool lake on a hot summer night as a way to encourage us to jump into the unknown. Otherwise, we end up choosing to experience life from the safe seats on the dock.

My hope for you is that you don't just dangle your feet in the water. I hope you dive in, embracing your unique ability to choose what's right for you.

Winning, Losing, Learning

It would be nice, right, if we only had to learn lessons once? If we came out a butterfly who never so much as nicked her wings again? But that isn't how it goes.

I wasn't sure I was ever going to be a mom. I wasn't even sure I was going to be a mom when I fell in love with my husband, Nick. I would have been happy living out our days just the two of us—I know it. But what other joy might we be missing if we skipped the parenting adventure together? We started to wonder.

When we got pregnant with Dorothy, I was in my late thirties and confident. Decisive. I was determined not to should the shit out of motherhood, starting with the baby shower.

I hate baby showers. Always have. (Truth be told, I hate showers of any nature. And while I'm at it, guess what? I don't love over-the-top kid birthday parties, either. Hate me if you must, but I don't think I'm alone.) So I wouldn't let my family or friends host one for me—let alone multiple showers.

Should number one—shed. I was winning.

Immediately after Dorothy was born, I set very clear boundaries. I wanted to be alone with my babe, and sometimes with myself. It was the coldest winter on record, and all I wanted to do was hole up and snuggle. It's what I needed, and I knew it. So when people asked to visit, I said no in no uncertain terms. Even to my closest friends. Tara, who was peed on alongside me that New Year's Eve in New York, was desperate to spoil us with love and gifts.

"Do not come," I said. "I don't want people here."

Then, a mutual friend of ours popped by unexpectedly to bring a gift and posted a photo. Tara didn't know the context—that the friend was an uninvited guest who I gently nudged out in ten minutes. But it didn't matter. She was furious because she was hurt.

Of course, we eventually apologized and patched things up, which is the beauty of longtime friendships. But you know what? I still have no regrets about creating those boundaries.

Should number two—shed. Parenting? I had it down. My kid. My happiness. My rules. Still winning.

Then came the wedding.

Dorothy was four months old, and one of Nick's lifelong friends was getting married in his hometown in Minnesota. A proud new daddy, Nick desperately wanted to introduce our sweet girl to his family and friends.

I, meanwhile, was in a dark hole I couldn't seem to climb out of. Despite hiring a lactation consultant who was with me every day, my breasts refused to produce more than an ounce or two of milk at a time. Sometimes less. Drink beer, people said. Eat more healthy fats. Give it another day. Another week. Another month. I did it all. I listened. I learned. I tried. I would nurse Dorothy on both breasts, and she'd get maybe half an ounce total. Then I would immediately set her down to start pumping, trying to trigger my body into giving milk. Sometimes, I'd get an ounce or two. Other times, I'd get nothing. I did it sixteen times a day on each side—thirty-two times every day. Then, as soon as I finished, I'd run to make formula for Dorothy since I wasn't producing enough milk to satisfy her appetite. In between, I would sit and sob.

I also felt deflated about my body. I didn't know at the time that I had a thyroid disease, and that there was medication to help regulate my weight. So I was eating well, working out, trying desperately to breastfeed, and not losing the weight I had put on while pregnant.

I knew going to the wedding was a should. You should go to the wedding. You should introduce the baby. You should smile and pretend that this is dreamy. You should make sure everyone knows just how perfect your family is. But the handsome man I married—the man I loved—wanted to take me on a date and show off our daughter. He deserved that, right? So I agreed to go.

I enlisted a stylist to put an outfit together, hoping that would help me feel less insecure about how I looked. And it did. Until we showed up at the rehearsal dinner. There was Nick's close friend

Sarah, a super fit nutritionist who had just birthed her third child. Her waistline was tiny, her muscles tight. "Oh my gosh, I woke up and pumped sixteen ounces!" she exclaimed, trying to make new-mom conversation and, in the process, unknowingly stabbing my heart. I scrambled back to our room to pump the moment the rehearsal dinner ended. Dry.

I hated every minute of that trip. I wasn't cute. I couldn't nourish my baby. I felt completely inadequate. Comparison is, in fact, the thief of joy.

Should number three—decidedly not shed. Losing. Big.

Know what I know now? Parenting is fucking hard.

When our second daughter, Maeve, was born, Dorothy was sixteen months old. Her little one-year-old self toddled into the hospital as Maeve was being bathed. Maeve was screaming, and Dorothy ran to me, scared. In that moment, I felt pure dread, realizing how difficult parenting a toddler and an infant was going to be. Back home, I started hating 4 p.m. It's when Dorothy's nanny left each day, and I would have to take care of both girls, often alone, for three hours—or, if Nick was traveling, all night. Sometimes when the clock struck four, I cried.

Because parenting is hard—and because life is hard—we're not always going to get it right. We're going to set boundaries we're proud of, and we're going to go to weddings we shouldn't. The best we can do is learn. And learn again. And learn better.

I once said no to box seats for my family at an event my kids would have gone bananas over. The person who extended the generous offer paused for a moment. "I am so impressed by your ability to be clear about what you are and are not willing to do," she said. It has taken me years to get good at saying no. But I now understand that every no I say to one thing gives me time and space to say yes to another. In this particular example, saying yes to this event with my family would have been saying no to prepping for a week of solo parenting. And heaven knows I'm over the days of crying at 4 p.m.

Also, pro tip: the quicker you shed a should, the better. I had one client experiencing classic symptoms of the disease to please. Someone asked her to get involved in a cause she's passionate about, but she was at max capacity with her current commitments. She let the email sit in her inbox for a week, taking up precious space in her mind. She wanted to say no but felt yes would be easier. She didn't want to disappoint them. I encouraged her to say no in a gracious and brief way (brief because so many times when we say no to something, we offer to do something we think will take up less time to be nice, and that usually backfires). I actually wrote a two-line email for her and encouraged her to decline the opportunity before leaving her office for the day. The result? She felt instant relief the moment she pressed send on the email. It lifted the mental load she'd been carrying around for days.

I will tell you what I told her and what I must keep reminding myself over and over and over again: you are not a vending machine. And no is a complete sentence.

LIVE THE LIFE YOU IMAGINED

Ah, expectations. We've all got them. For relationships. For kids. For work. For life.

And reality doesn't often match those expectations, does it?

The holidays are a great example. As we review our overeating, our overspending, and our overscheduling, we promise that next year is going to be better. Then there we are again, putting on those extra pounds we worked so hard to get off, stressed from searching for the perfect gifts, barking at the kids to get in the car so we can get to Grandma's before we hop over to Aunt Susie's.

We often wind up there because we don't want to disappoint others. We don't want to turn down party invites from clients. We don't want to give what we perceive to be a subpar gift. We don't want to sadden Grandma and Aunt Susie.

Friends, Henry James said it best: *it's time to start living the life you imagined.*

Consider this: when we put necessary boundaries in place, we often upset others—but end up creating a better experience for those who matter most.

Deciding to spend Christmas morning at home with my husband and daughters, for example, means our extended families don't see us until later that day. But it creates a more intimate and memorable experience for us. Another example: last year, I stopped seeing clients on Thursdays. It meant less money in the short term, yes. But it gave me priceless space for things I love: class with my favorite yoga instructor, time to write, and an opportunity to breathe.

If your reality is not aligning with your expectations, I invite you to ask yourself these two simple questions:

1. **How do I want to feel?** Identify the feelings you want to experience over the next few months, the next couple of weeks, or even just for the day.

2. **What makes me feel that way?** Consider what makes you feel what you want to feel, and make sure you're scheduling time for it. Baby steps are great; five minutes might be where you start. So start there.

It's time to start experiencing the life you imagined. Today.

A Date with Me

The first time I ever dined alone was at a mall in Maryland. I was a nineteen-year-old college junior interning on Capitol Hill. I spent long days with the super sexy House Budget Committee. I had no life and no network. One weekend, I went shopping and then walked into a restaurant by myself. I sat down with a book, so nervous I was shaking. I'm not sure I felt liberated by meal's end, but I at least survived.

The next time I did something society suggests you shouldn't do alone, I was just out of school living in Hoboken. I took the train into Manhattan on a Saturday. I went mostly window shopping but bought something for my apartment at Bed Bath & Beyond—a bedspread, maybe, because I remember toting that giant plastic bag all over. I picked a restaurant and didn't shake as I ate by myself.

Then, on a whim, I decided to see a movie. Inside the theater, I positioned that giant bag in the seat beside me. It felt so nerve-racking, and then so glorious. So much so that I decided to go to another movie afterward. Back to back! I rode the train home to Hoboken on a high. I felt so free.

I took my first solo vacation to Vieques, a tiny Caribbean island off of Puerto Rico's eastern coast with blue-green water, magnificent sunsets, and little else. On my first night there, I hopped onto a barstool at El Quenepo. Tim, a fifty-something investment banker from Chicago, joined on one side. He was having marital problems and dreamed of opening a boating business. Then came Ralph, a retired banking executive in his seventies from Boston. He kept joints in his socks and had never traveled by himself until now. We decided to meet again the next night. We ended up having three dinners together—including on Valentine's Day, when they treated me.

Before we said goodbye, we committed to dreams we'd make happen before the next Valentine's Day rolled around. I promised to train for a Muay Thai fight. Tim said he'd open his boat business. And Ralph vowed to travel on his own again. We stayed in touch. And all three of us kept our promises. Tim even reconciled with his wife.

After Amal and I broke up, I returned to Vieques alone again. The eight-person puddle jumper from San Juan to Vieques included a group of adorable boys from Boston who were headed to the island for a wedding and me. I knew before that plane took off I'd be invited. Sure as shit, by the time we landed, I was heading to the rehearsal dinner with them for pizza and beer at an open-air bar called Jack's. Fun as it was, I passed on their invitation to the wedding. But I ran into them all week. Back then, getting a car on the island was tough. You had to reserve one in advance and take what you got. Mine had no door handles on the inside and no mirrors. (It did have a seat belt, though, which was quite a luxury.)

I ran into the Boston boys one day as they searched for the famous black beach. Fuck it, I thought. I'll go too. Hiking to a secluded beach with four strange men probably wasn't a wise idea, but I did it anyway. We hiked, swam, drank, and then hiked back to where we'd started. I offered to give them a ride to their rental house. As we drove, I nodded toward the missing handles and joked that everyone was locked in now. Ironically, this single woman from Ohio successfully scared the hell out of four grown-ass men. They panicked. I laughed. We all had to roll down the windows to open the doors from the outside to get out.

Now, even with a built-in forever date, two kiddos, and an amazing group of friends, I still love going to the movies by myself. For an occasional treat, I'll leave Nick home with the girls and dine alone at a bar. And once every year or two, I'll take a solo vacation.

Marriage, motherhood, even work teams—they all make it easy to forget who we are. Returning to that—returning to me—has always been how I ground myself. How I refocus. How I refuel. It brings me joy.

It's funny how I feel like I need to put a disclaimer here. I love my husband! I love my kids! I love being with all of my people! It's yet another should, right? The need to explain to people what you're not sure they'll understand because we should all want to be with our people all of the time. And all of those statements—all of those loves—are true.

But I also love being a party of one. And you know what? It's not just okay. It's magic.

CHAPTER THREE

Remaking My Bed
{Prioritize. Evolve. Repeat.}

*"Twenty years from now, you will be more
disappointed by the things that you didn't
do than by the ones you did do. So throw
off the bowlines. Sail away from the safe
harbor. Catch the trade winds in your
sails. Explore. Dream. Discover."*

—Unknown, but frequently attributed to Mark Twain

I was sad, and I was scared. I had just told Mark I wanted a
divorce and was sitting in my office that week when my very
disappointed brother Peter called. He started yelling as soon as
I picked up.

"Look, I'm going through a hard time," I said. "I'm feeling
really sad."

"Good," he said. "You need to sleep in the bed you made."

What the hell?

That phrase might be my least favorite one, ever. Because here's the thing: you make your bed every single day. Every day. Which means that every day, you have a chance to start over. To make your bed differently. Or to make it better. Or to wash the sheets. Or to buy a whole new fucking bed.

I've made and remade many beds—in my relationships, in my career, in how I parent the daughters I love. We evolve, and our priorities must evolve with us.

First case in point: my divorce. Conjuring up the nerve to do it took nearly all I had. Then, the Catholic Church, to which I had been faithful for my entire life and whose house so clearly hasn't been in order for decades, sent me a letter disowning me. It felt like the deepest form of betrayal—one from which I will never recover. And while I'm not fully sure about faith at this point, I do believe that Jesus supports remaking beds. I mean, isn't the whole point of His existence on earth because humans mess up? He came to say, "It's okay. I've got you." Right? Regardless, remaking my bed meant losing the only religion I had ever known. But any religion that castigates and expels people for asking out of lifelong promises they made far too young isn't the one for me anyway. No regrets.

While I never liked what my marriage bed looked like from the beginning, there are other beds I've made that I really celebrated—for a while. There was a time in my life, for example, when I found my dream job. It was a position to establish the brand and identity for an upstart nonprofit. I helped build a camp for children with serious illnesses that earned a rare induction into a network of camps founded by late actor Paul Newman. I worked tireless hours, crafting marketing plans from nine to five, entertaining donors at events until the wee hours, and then sleeping in bunk beds on camp weekends. And I loved it. As in, pinched-myself-every-morning loved it. Until I didn't.

A few years in, what had been my dream job became my nemesis. I was, by then, happily married to Nick. The hour-long drive (each way) that once made me smile because I was headed to a dreamy paradise now just meant two fewer hours a day with my man. The evening events that once lit me up now felt like they were simply date-night thieves. The tiny team I once helped lead had grown into a larger one with a menagerie of personalities and complicated politics. One day, the team decided we were hosting two events in two different zip codes on the same day. I made my best case for why the idea was terrible. I was outvoted.

Clearly, my priorities had evolved, and I needed to, too. I created my exit plan accordingly.

And it's taboo to say, but you know what? Right now, my daughters are not my priority. My work is. That doesn't mean I love my girls any less than the next mom. Or that I don't intentionally carve out space to be with them and enjoy them. Or that I don't teach them and tuck them in and relish precious everyday moments. It simply means that after making them my priority for the first few years of their lives—and shortening my work hours accordingly—I recalibrated. My husband embraced it. And I gave myself permission to work longer hours, to accept more opportunities to travel, to hire more help, and to give more energy to a career that brings me a lot of fulfillment.

We only have to sleep in the bed we made this morning tonight. Tomorrow's a whole new day.

HOW DO YOU FIND HAPPINESS? START HERE.

We're human. Which means we're prone to restlessness and reevaluation.

Don't fight it, friends. Embrace it. Use it.

Maybe you're considering making a career change. Perhaps you're overwhelmed but simultaneously bored. Or you might just feel unsettled in a way you can't quite place.

Enter the life audit.

I walk all of my clients through this exercise when we meet. It's all about assessing who you want to be.

We start by taking a holistic view of your life and evaluating eight areas that make up the life wheel:

- Family
- Work
- Money
- Personal growth
- Health and wellness
- Spirituality
- Community
- Living environment

We rank areas according to importance, and then we rank them according to the amount of time you realistically devote to each area.

In her *Harvard Business Review* article "Steps to Take When You're Starting to Feel Burned Out," executive coach Monique Valcour offers this strategy: for one week, track what you're doing during blocks of time each day. Then, note the value of each activity and how it makes you feel. Angry? Depressed? Joyful? Energized?

"The basic principle is to limit your exposure to the tasks, people, and situations that drain you," Valcour says, "and increase your exposure to those that replenish you."

Sometimes, simply identifying your priorities versus your realities is enlightening. For example, you might want family to rank first. But in reality, family ranks fifth. Wish they were number one? Strategize steps to get there. Once you start taking them, happiness follows.

Try it for yourself: which four areas would you say are your top priorities now? Which four do you wish were your top priorities?

Your answers to these two questions could reveal the source of your restlessness.

Maybe you're putting a lot of time and energy into a job that doesn't seem to be furthering your personal growth. Or perhaps your health and wellness have taken a backseat to community obligations.

When we're able to clearly define what it is we want, we establish our core values—those things that we say are most important to us. If our actions aren't aligning with our core values, then we shouldn't be surprised to feel anxious and uptight.

Once you're able to say, "OK, I see where I'm falling short, and I want to make a change," you can create an action plan. This is a set of specific, intentional, manageable steps to get you to a better, happier place.

That may mean setting aside twenty minutes to go on a walk a few times a week. Or maybe it's spending an hour updating your resume to reflect your most recent accomplishments.

Just creating this plan can do wonders for your restlessness. You're already being truer to who you are and what you want.

Happiness isn't elusive. It's possible. You simply need to define what it means to you—and enjoy the journey.

Blood

I can picture it so vividly—my brother Mike and I huddled inside our homemade family room fort, listening to Bruce Springsteen on a cassette player, singing lyrics we didn't fully understand.

The music of my siblings became the soundtrack of my life. The Boss. The Beatles. Tom Petty. The Rolling Stones. We listened to it on long road trips when I sat in the way back of the wood-paneled family station wagon. We listened to it in the yard when friends came over for cookouts. We listened to it in their bedrooms, where they occasionally let their baby sister pop in and hang.

We lived in a ranch house, sharing one bathroom among most of us. (My parents eventually added one in the basement, meaning they only had to share their bathroom with three kids rather than six.) And it wasn't South of Lane, as people liked to ask. We drove old cars. And I didn't know what The Gap was until sixth grade.

Meaning we definitely weren't as ritzy as many of the folks around us. But what we lacked in money, we more than made up for in love, and in warmth, and in fun.

We worshipped in church every Sunday and prayed before dinner, which we ate together every night. Faith was our foundation, and it was a good one. We were raised to give, and my parents showed the way, opening their home for everyone from priests to the same group of twenty-five kids who streamed in weekly to watch the sitcom *Cheers*.

My siblings are a motley crew—one I cherish, despite our sometimes shockingly different political mindsets.

I was three when Ann, the oldest Walsh kid, went to college to become a teacher. She was bubbly and fun, with a near-photographic memory. She was much like a mother to me. So her absence was such a loss. Christmas breaks were the best because Ann was back. When she got married, I was eight. I thought we'd throw a big party, dance, eat cake, and then go back home together to enjoy the rest of the summer. I didn't realize she'd be driving off for her honeymoon and then moving to St. Louis to start her life until the reception ended. There's a photo of me in my pretty flower girl dress with baby's breath in my hair, holding on to Ann's gown for dear life. When she and her husband pulled away, I sobbed.

A couple of times, my parents put me on an airplane alone for solo trips to visit Ann. She had an apricot tree, so we picked apricots and figured out how to make apricot fruit roll-ups. During one trip, she bought me a skirt and sweater. I proudly wore that outfit on the first day of second grade, despite the fact it was a sweltering summer day and the sweater was wool. Ann's husband says she is always the most interesting person in the room, and he's right. Even now, I look forward to our summer vacations together, when we wait for the kids to go to sleep and Ann cooks a gourmet dinner for the adults, and we talk and drink and laugh and carry on.

Next in line is Pat—a staunch and proud conservative. He's so Republican, in fact, that one day when I was eleven and my friends and I made fun of him for mowing the lawn in dweeby tube socks, he barked back, "Get a job!" In college, he studied abroad in Luxembourg and then landed an internship in London. He would return to the States, but never home for good. I used to cry in my bedroom because I missed him. I was so very sensitive about my siblings leaving. I relished being together.

After I quit the job at the marketing firm, Pat invited me to spend a week with him and his three young boys in Chicago while his wife was away. He needed help; I needed money. It was a generous offer. One night over dinner, I told him I was dating a woman. "I'd rather you be a lesbian than a Democrat," he said. Yet somehow, he accepted that I was both.

After I left, Pat—the one most concerned about me after Dad died—wrote a note that I still have. *Dad is sitting with God in heaven, smiling down on you*, he said. *And you are perfect in his eyes.*

Peter is number three. He's six feet six, and he would chase my friends down the hallway and tickle us. He was the only Walsh kid who took an interest in the family business, which he now runs, so by the time I was in middle school, he was back in Columbus. He would take me to the Chef-o-Nette diner and attend my basketball games—always while wearing a giant plastic button with my photo. "This," he would brag, "is my sister."

Once Peter and his now-wife started dating, they took me on dates together. When they got married, I made buttons with Peter's photo and handed them out at the rehearsal dinner. So all of these guests showed up to the wedding wearing their buttons. It was perfect.

It was actually Peter who dropped me off at college. Dad was president of his industry's largest association, and he and Mom were in Europe for the annual association conference. So Peter and his wife drove me to school, treated me to lunch, took me to the bookstore to buy books and snacks, and waved goodbye. I was equal parts horrified that I was the only kid not hugging my parents and grateful I had such a great big brother.

It was also Peter, however, who made that nasty call upon discovering I was leaving Mark—the one who told me I needed to sleep in the bed I'd made. I suppose it's why sibling relationships are so special: because you can tell them to fuck off and know they'll never actually fuck off too far. Even if you sometimes want them to.

The fourth Walsh kid is Molly, a justice-seeker who stands up for the underdog, makes a mean mac 'n' cheese, and definitely knows how to have a good time. We shared a bedroom. I idolized her. And yes, I melted down when she left for college, too. Loss after loss, people!

From her dorm room at Miami of Ohio, Molly was thoughtful enough to make up sweet games we could play from afar. She wrote me letters, and we created little challenges, like, "Who will eat mashed potatoes first?" And then she would call and say, "I had mashed potatoes in the dining hall today!" When she came home, she would pick me up from elementary school on the tandem bicycle toting Long John donuts, which came darn close to making up for leaving me in the first place. The day she got her wisdom teeth pulled, I was so anxious that she was hurting that I threw up at school and had to go home early.

When I was in college, Molly and I drank together. We even looked enough alike despite our nine-year age gap that she would let me use her ID to get into this bar she liked. Then, as soon as I was in, I would walk out to the patio and pass the ID back to her through a fence so she could join.

Also, just so you don't think she's perfect, my deep-rooted fear of cicadas—these disgusting underground bugs that emerge every seventeen years—is because Molly once put a cicada shell on my pillow. I still have PTSD from that experience.

Mike, number five, is the siblingest of my siblings—the one just two years older who I grew up building forts with and going to school with. We were the kids who went all out for spirit days in high school, dressing in our '70s gear and picking up donuts and juice before school to serve to everyone in the junior parking lot. Once, when I was walking along the sidewalk, he slowed his car, and his friends opened the back door and motioned me in. As soon as I got there, Mike sped up. Then slowed to let me in. Then sped up again. Asshole.

Mike was a camp counselor for years—everyone's favorite, always.

He, too, was pissed about my divorce. And when he found out I was dating a woman, he was livid. "When I call Mom to tell her about Amal," he said, "what do you want me to say?" (I ended up driving to Mom's to tell her myself. I shook as I walked to the door. And guess what? She was an absolute champ.)

Mike is also the funniest person I know. Exhibit A: at one point, I had depleted my savings and was seriously struggling to pay my bills. As I drove home the first day of April during a spring storm, I started to cry. I prayed for answers, for help. When I pulled into my condo, there was a FedEx envelope at my door. My aunt had recently passed away, and inside the envelope was a copy of her will. Because she had no children, she had generously left her money to her sister, nieces, and nephews. Each of us kids would receive $25,000. I sat on my steps and sobbed—this time, tears of joy. It was an absolute shock, an answer to my desperate prayers. Everything was going to be okay. I called my Mike.

"I can't believe this happened," I wept. "Aunt Pat was amazing."

He agreed.

"But wait," he said. "Did you see the paragraph about Mom and the snaggletooth cat?"

I looked more closely. I noticed that one of the attorneys listed was Ohio State's football coach. *No. No. No. No. No.*

This, friends, was a masterful April Fools' Day joke by my brother—the very one I had called to share the good news with. Well played, Mike. And fuck you.

These people—a couple of them can be dicks. They know that. But they sure did introduce me to good music. And even if they haven't always liked how I make—or remake—my bed, they have never stopped showing up. I love them fiercely. I still cry when they leave.

LIVE BY DESIGN, NOT DEFAULT

Live by design, not default.

I've read this in a few different places. And each time, it's caused me to consider what it really means to live by default and, more importantly, what a life by design requires.

A life of default decisions sounds incredibly boring, right? To act based on a plan made for you instead of by you puts you in a place of learned helplessness and requires little courage or creativity. What kind of personal growth could come from a life like that?

A life by design sounds much more fulfilling to me. But it demands something substantial: authority.

Owning your authority means proudly asserting the power you have over your own life. It means that once you've mapped out your goals and priorities, you live them out with intention. It means courage.

When I meet with clients who struggle to own their authority, I ask them to consider these three points.

If you ignore your dreams long enough, they'll go silent.
Shauna Niequist reminds us of this in her book *Present Over Perfect*. It's the tragic tale of those passions and dreams that go ignored and avoided in the name of life by default. Eventually, they stop pursuing you, too.

I have two clients who constantly put off making decisions because they're waiting on X to happen. I'll stay until I have a baby. I'll leave once the perfect opportunity comes along.

What are you telling yourself by living in this place of if? Trust yourself enough to act now, knowing your dreams won't keep knocking.

Don't operate in someone else's space.
My brother Mike—along with more than 1,000 other applicants—wanted to drive the Oscar Mayer Wienermobile. In his application, he promised that, if given an interview, he would send an autographed copy of his senior portrait. He got the interview. As promised, he sent an autographed, eight-by-ten senior pic—in which he was wearing gross novelty teeth. Then, he showed up for his interview wearing the teeth. He took them out near the end and got the gig. Which was perfect for him.

I, on the other hand, have been to many an interview for jobs that weren't exactly a fit. I once walked into an interview at a Fortune 20 company where each associate wears a name badge she has to swipe like every seven steps. I was, quite literally, textured tights in a nude pantyhose world. "What's your biggest fear in taking this job?" my interviewer asked. I didn't even try to mask my feelings. "Accepting a job I have no desire to do," I said. They didn't call back. Obviously.

Not only did I stick to my core values in that situation, I freed up what was likely an ideal opportunity for someone else. Had I stayed, I would've been begrudgingly operating in that person's space.

It's a selfish way to live. So when the fear of taking risks comes around, comfort yourself with the idea that you're giving another person the chance to live their best life. Your Oscar Mayer Wienermobile is waiting somewhere else.

You can't be taken advantage of.
I once received an email from a friend who was worried about his wife. She was working seventy-hour weeks for a boss who was taking all the credit. She was burned out and exhausted, causing her husband to worry about their family's future.

He encouraged her to reach out to me, which she promised she'd do in a few days after her current projects were completed. That was two years ago.

The truth is we give people the advantage by actively choosing to be victims of our circumstances. That's a life by default, friends.

That woman doesn't have to live a life by default. In this woman's life by design, I see her approaching her boss with purpose and confidence, setting boundaries, and managing expectations. I see her owning her authority. And I see happiness resulting.

Are you living by default or design? If it's not the latter, it can be.

Design away.

Passion Play

Emily Lewis was nine years old when she walked downstairs and told her mother there was blood in the toilet.

A cancerous tumor had spread across her insides and into her lungs.

But she smiled her way through treatments. In the hospital, she raced wheelchairs and used her IV stand as a skateboard. Outside of the hospital, she continued practicing Taekwondo and shined bright on stage for an American Cancer Society fundraiser. "If this speech sounds like I'm making it up as I go," she told the crowd, "it's because I am." A wake of laughter and smiles followed wherever she ventured.

Emily's rigorous chemotherapy and radiation treatments started working. The cancer was regressing. As it did, a nurse suggested Emily try something new. A group was building a camp called Flying Horse Farms in Ohio for kids with serious illnesses, she explained. While they fundraised to do it, they were sending Ohio children to similar camps out of state.

A week away from home? Emily hadn't spent a single night away from Mom since her diagnosis. She wasn't sure what a week apart would feel like. But she wanted to find out.

The Hole in the Wall Gang Camp is a Wild West-themed camp in Connecticut founded by actor Paul Newman. He was inspired to open it after visiting a friend with cancer in the hospital and feeling crushed by the weight the children with the disease were carrying. Wouldn't it be great, he thought, if there was a place they could go to just be kids? Somewhere they could raise a little hell? He vowed to build it himself. The Hole in the Wall Gang Camp became the first camp of what is now the SeriousFun Children's Network. It includes about fifteen brick-and-mortar camps and myriad programs worldwide serving children with serious illnesses and their families. Every camp is free of charge.

And by summertime, Emily was at the airport, hugging her parents goodbye to go.

At camp, other kids were bald, too, with equally ravaged insides. With a hospital conspicuously onsite and specialists doubling as camp counselors looking on, the kids caught fish. Shot arrows. Crafted masterpieces. Shared secrets. Sang songs. Meanwhile, instead of logging miles on the treadmill—like all parents navigating a child's illness, she had to stay close—Emily's mom got to run outside. Instead of hustling to appointments for her daughter, she and her husband got to focus on their son. It was, they said, a gift. And Emily returned with newfound friends, upgraded joy, and a red, blue, and yellow quilt that she wouldn't let go. She had only one round of chemotherapy to complete her protocol. Life was looking up.

But a few months later, Emily's cancer had returned. After it was evident that traditional chemotherapies weren't affecting her cancer, her family began logging thousands of miles traveling from Cleveland to Cincinnati and as far as Washington, DC, for clinical trials. Emily was game for anything, she said, as long as she got to return to camp. It was, she told doctors, not negotiable.

She returned to Hole in the Wall giddy with excitement. For that one week, she felt free from her disease. Her family did, too, taking their own well-deserved vacation. It was like a big, collective breath to gear them up for another year of travel and treatments. Inhale. Smile. Sing. Laugh. Dance. Exhale.

The next summer, Flying Horse Farms, the Ohio camp, was breaking ground. Camp leaders scheduled Emily to speak at the ceremony alongside her father. She would fly to The Hole in the Wall Gang Camp immediately after.

Emily counted down the days. She carefully packed her camp T-shirts and shorts into her red bag. Her parents loaded it into the car. One last, quick hospital treatment, she thought, and then on to the groundbreaking and camp. Let's. Go.

But at the hospital, something wasn't right. Fluid kept filling Emily's left lung, despite doctors draining it. Discomfort turned to severe pain. Doctors ordered more tests. As the groundbreaking neared, Emily's father said he wasn't going.

"What are you talking about, Dad?" Emily said. "You have to go to camp. You have to do the groundbreaking. You have to get camp open."

So he went, and he told people about his little girl. About the independence and joy camp brought her. About the respite it brought the family.

Back at the hospital, doctors realized that what they thought was fluid was cancer. And it was everywhere.

She died at home two months later, never having made it back to camp.

Stories like Emily's are what lured me to Flying Horse Farms. After becoming One-Week Walsh, working part-time for the family business, and draining my savings account while trying to find work that would give me life, camp was worth the wait. The Flying Horse Farms CEO, a legendary power player who took the camp position as her encore, hired me to be Chief Storytelling Officer. I was charged with creating the brand from scratch. Core values. Website. Pamphlets. Press packets.

It was like a gift-wrapped dream straight from the heavens.

The freedom that camp gave kids like Emily—it was a true privilege to be part of a place that could do that. And so, as camp's buildings went up and the pool went in and the website went live, it felt surreal. It felt satisfying. It felt like I had found my purpose in the world.

Before we opened camp, we hosted a trial weekend for family and friends. As timing would have it, however, the SeriousFun gala was that Thursday night in New York City. It's a swanky, star-studded event that draws A-list celebrities and, most importantly, cash for the cause. On top of that, we, as the new kids in town trying to earn accreditation into the network, were hosting a private party that I was overseeing. The CEO, development director, and I worked the rooms like champs. Then, I chugged some water to avoid a hangover I couldn't afford, slept for a few hours, escaped Manhattan for an early morning flight, landed in Columbus, changed into shorts, and made the hour-long drive to camp in time for lunch. I headed straight to the kitchen, where reps from the company that had outfitted the space taught us how to use the equipment. We then scrambled to make the bunk beds before our guests arrived.

By the time our campers checked in and dinner rolled around, we couldn't remember how to turn on the ovens to bake the lasagna. After an inordinate amount of swearing and a miraculous save, we cooked, served, cleaned, and laughed until midnight, when I crawled into my uncomfortable bunk and listened to weird noises on the walkie-talkie that I wasn't allowed to turn off. I woke at 5:30 a.m. to prep breakfast. I was troubleshooting equipment and washing dishes in an old prom dress—because, camp!—unknowingly violating codes left and right. I was then responsible for coming up with a craft. On the fly. I think we tried to make slime. I'm sure it failed.

It was a shit show. But it was our shit show. And I knew that eventually, it was going to change lives.

It did.

There was the little girl with a giant scar across her chest where doctors had transplanted her heart. She had always worn a shirt over her swimsuit in public, embarrassed, unwilling to answer the inevitable questions. Until camp, where all of the children in her session shared the same scar.

There was the shy kid who, in his first year, conjured up the guts to perform in the talent show, albeit behind a makeshift curtain that counselors held. By his last summer, he was in a camp band.

There was the sweet boy with a brain tumor in his head, braces on his legs, and a complicated life at home. At camp, he rode around in the golf cart from activity to activity, beaming, king of the world.

There was the mom who came to a family camp and spent the bulk of the weekend slowly swaying back and forth in a rocking chair on her cabin's porch. I stopped by and sat in the chair beside her. She worked two jobs, I learned, always scrambling to get her child to doctor's appointments and manage medication between. She never had an opportunity to rest her bones.

"This," she said, "is the best weekend I've ever had."

At the end of each session, watching the campers clutch each other as they hugged goodbye could bring you to your knees. I would pray they would be alive to return. Not all of them would. But they all would hold onto camp. To its empowerment. To its joy.

Doing that work was the biggest honor of my life, and I mean that with every fiber of my being.

But after a handful of years, I began running out of steam. I was coordinating pamphlets, videos, and events by day. Slipping on dresses and heels for fundraisers by night. Making beds and prepping cabins on Fridays. Cooking, cleaning, and crafting during camp sessions. And then starting over again, always with an hour-long commute each way.

As camp grew, so, too, did the staff and, inevitably, office politics. Plus, I had not only met and started dating Nick, I had married him. I began dreading the drive the moment my eyes opened in the morning.

Then, in that woeful meeting that fateful day, the team decided we were hosting back-to-back fundraisers, despite my arguments against the idea.

"It's insane," one person said, "but doable."

For them, maybe. But not for me. I marked the dates on my calendar and immediately began crafting a plan to exit before those dates arrived. The next morning, I woke up, spread the curtains, and started to sing.

Nick smiled from bed.

"You're back," he said.

The funny thing is I never realized just how far from me I had gotten. What had for so long served my soul had started eating it. My priority was no longer giving my entire existence to work that mattered. It was doing fulfilling work while also having the time and emotional bandwidth to nurture a marriage with the man I loved. Once I recognized that my priorities had evolved and I shifted accordingly, my entire aura changed. Within hours.

Last summer, Flying Horse Farms invited me back to speak to a group of Rangers—kids who have aged out of camp but aren't old enough to be counselors. I laughed and cried for the entire fifty-five-mile drive from my front door to camp's gate. So many memories.

Of all the work I've done, I may still be most proud of the ten core values I helped camp create. The best one?

Fearless is free.

In other words, friends, be brave. And when you no longer like the bed you made, trash the whole damn thing and buy a new one.

CHAPTER FOUR

Grapefruit on the Toilet
{Ask for What You Need}

*"You get in life what you have
the courage to ask for."*
—Oprah Winfrey

On my first real date with Nick, I arrived at the restaurant early. It was packed. As I squeezed between people to find a place to wait, I saw a dentist I had been on a couple of dates with. He smiled, excited to see me.

"I'm meeting a friend," I lied. "But it's crowded, so we'll go somewhere else."

He and his friends had secured a few seats at the bar.

"Why don't you just join us?" he offered.

I panicked and started spinning a web. I walked outside to wait for Nick, who, once he arrived, was anxious to get out of the rain and into the restaurant.

"No," I said, leaving him under the awning, wet. "You wait right here."

I went back to the dentist. Spin, spin, spin. Then I walked out to Nick and did the same until he and I were at another restaurant, and I was all sorts of distraught.

"I'm sorry," I finally said. "I haven't heard anything you've said for the last twenty minutes. Here's the deal..."

I spilled it: the awkward run-in with the dentist, the lies I had told Nick until he agreed to a different restaurant. I didn't want to start our relationship—however long it might last—with anything but total honesty. We laughed, and laughed, and laughed, and we haven't stopped for eight years.

The real win is that I wasn't just honest that night; I decided I would be honest about my boundaries and needs, come what may. I told Nick I hated talking on the phone. Unlike Spring Fling, his predecessor, he respected that boundary. I told him I'd only go out twice a week. He respected that boundary, too. And as our lives evolve and my boundaries shift, he respects them every step of the way.

It's perhaps the key reason our relationship works so well: we both ask for what we need, and we always deliver for each other.

It's not just critical to a good marriage. It's critical to a good life.

Everything that's ever been worth having has required me to ask for what I needed.

Bottom line: if you can't communicate what you want, you'll probably never get it. That includes asking yourself for what you need, too. Then listening. And delivering.

TAKING TIME OFF? SET BOUNDARIES.

It was her first vacation in quite a long time.

My client was telling me about her strategy for her time off: an approach that she had determined would help her enjoy her trip while still allowing her to stay in the work loop.

"I'm just going to check my email twice a day," she said.

Just? I was flummoxed.

Taking time off, after all, insinuates a need to unplug. And doing so allows us to have richer, more meaningful experiences away from our everyday responsibilities. But, as was the case with my client, it's often not realistic to entirely disengage while you're away. That's why, in this age of constant connectedness, it's important to set boundaries when you're preparing for time off.

So I'll give you the same advice I gave her.

Before you leave, send status updates.
Back when I was managing all the communication and culture for the nonprofit, I took a trip to Paris. On a previous trip, I had learned firsthand how checking in with work can ruin a vacation, so I knew I wanted to leave work and really *leave* work.

Before I set my out-of-office message, I took stock of my projects and sent status updates to the folks who might have questions while I was away. It gave me peace of mind to know that all parties were informed and up to date.

Fib on your outgoing message.
Being totally off the grid wasn't an option for my client. But that didn't mean she needed to broadcast her availability. She was

definitely going to check in from time to time, but I recommended that her out-of-office say that she was offline.

That way, colleagues who emailed her with nonurgent questions would have a realistic expectation of when she might respond. And she could feel comfortable knowing they were aware of that delay.

Ask your direct reports for a recap.
Tell those who report to you to send you a briefing on the day before you return, with info on anything you've missed. (And try to stay off email until then.) Those recaps will arm you with the intelligence you need as you transition back into your routine.

This is also a great way to instill trust in your team. You're letting them know you believe they can handle things while you're away, and that's empowering.

I'm happy to report that my client took my advice, checking her email once mid-vacation and once right before her return.

"It was actually easy and very freeing for me," she said. "My team and my assistant all did a great job of supporting me."

That, my friends, is a win.

LAKE CHAMPION

The camp was stunning. A glimmering lake tucked inside acres of lush, green trees. Sturdy wooden cabins carefully built into a charming little community. Big pool. Tall waterslides. Colorful flowers.

I went to Lake Champion, a Christian camp in upstate New York, to volunteer for a month between my junior and senior years of high school. I worked fourteen- to sixteen-hour days in the dining hall, where we filled countless pitchers of water and juice, folded linen napkins for three meals a day, and meticulously placed knives and forks at each seat, *as if each and every setting were for Jesus.* It was the kind of place where soul-searching was welcome and listening to Indigo Girls on the boom box was not. (Learned that lesson the hard way. Because, you know, lesbians are bad.)

One night, one of our leaders, a kind man from Connecticut, shared a testimony about his struggle with depression.

Wait, I thought. That sadness, his sadness—I knew that. I felt that.

I waited for the right moment and approached his wife. I told her how I always felt sad, even when there wasn't a reason to. How I was exhausted all the time. How I would go into my room to hide and cry.

She set up a time for Dave and me to talk.

We sat on an old wooden picnic table, looking at all of those tall, tall trees, hundreds of years in the making, and I tried to turn my feelings, my silent struggles, into words. He understood, he said. He told me how he got help, how he was living a really happy life now. He offered to introduce me to his therapist, and when I accepted, he reached out to her and set up a call.

Once I was home, I talked to Dave's therapist on the phone. Then we arranged a call with my mom. I told Mom there was someone I wanted her to talk to. I was in the basement on one phone, and my mom was upstairs in her bedroom on another. The therapist explained why we were talking, and then I hung up and let them continue. I had never heard the term mental illness; people didn't openly discuss it then—at least not where I lived.

I wasn't sure how Mom would take any of this. I certainly didn't want her, or anybody, to feel like they'd messed up. But I was broken, and if there was a way out of this, I wanted to find it. It was as high as I knew how to raise my hand at seventeen.

I don't know what Mom said to Dad. But a couple of weeks later, on a Friday night, my parents sat on the couch watching *The McLaughlin Group* on TV. I was heading out the door for a high school football game when Dad stopped me with his voice.

"Regan," Dad said, "you have nothing to be depressed about."

I smiled softly. He wasn't trying to be cruel, I knew. He was killing himself to give me this life—this beautiful, laugh-fueled, love-filled life. And in theory, of course, I had nothing to be depressed about. He just didn't understand. He couldn't understand.

"OK," I said. And then I walked out the door.

Mom didn't understand either, but she got me help nonetheless. I started seeing a therapist and taking antidepressants. Over time, I figured out that a lot of what I was feeling was rooted in deep shame and self-doubt, related to not feeling smart enough or good enough—not feeling like I was mentally capable of keeping up in my school's competitive environment.

I was on and off the antidepressants from seventeen to twenty-eight. I used the therapist briefly as a teen. Later, as a young adult, I found another one I adored, and I have talked with her throughout my life when I need support. Sometimes that's twice a month, and sometimes I go years without visiting. The last time I went was when I was eight months pregnant with Maeve and wanted guidance on how to manage an impending visit from my in-laws. The idea of having them in the house for several days with our toddler and a newborn baby, trying to navigate breastfeeding all over again, felt overwhelming. (The session result? I humbly asked Nick's parents if they would mind staying in a hotel. Thank you, Ginny and Bill, for being so understanding.)

I feel lucky because I haven't dealt with symptoms of my depression in over twelve years. Sure, I have moments when I don't feel as much sizzle. But it doesn't knock me to my knees. And not always being happy? That's life. Not feeling amazing is far different from being depressed. Exercise and healthy eating, I've also learned, are critical to my mental health.

There's so much I wish I could tell my seventeen-year-old self. But mostly this: way to go, girl. I'm really fucking proud of you.

OUT OF STORAGE?
HERE ARE THREE WAYS TO RESTORE SOME SPACE.

You're almost out of storage.

You've gotten that warning message before, right? Perhaps it pops up on your phone or in your inbox.

You knew it was coming—things were moving slower than usual, and small tasks were much more difficult. But there just wasn't time to manage the influx of messages, media, and storage-snatching data.

That's where we all sometimes get—figuratively speaking, of course.

For me, it often happens in February. The holidays have come and gone, as have my daughter's birthday and a steady stream of family visits, plus plenty of work travel. I can feel my storage nearing capacity, and I need to take some small steps to declutter.

Of course, the warning messages aren't quite as obvious in our day-to-day lives. It's up to us to determine if we're almost out of space.

Perhaps you've found yourself being short with the people around you. Or you've missed a deadline or a detail you normally wouldn't. Maybe you just feel *blah*.

Try one (or all) of these tips to restore some space.

Be honest. Sometimes simply telling someone—a colleague, spouse, or friend—what we're feeling can be therapeutic enough to free up some room. Our minds are chock full of info, and we often assume that others inherently know what we're thinking or feeling. We have to remember: they have their own storage issues. Speak up, and be clear about whether you're seeking advice or simply a listening ear.

Change it up. Do something radical or out of the norm. I recently went to see a movie with a friend on a Sunday after-noon, a time I usually reserve for family. I hadn't done it in years. Breaking free from my routine gave me some pep in my step and a fresh perspective. Try taking a walk at lunch instead of working through it. Enjoy a concert on a weeknight. Schedule a spontaneous trip.

Say yes with caution. This goes for personal opportunities and professional opportunities—and I know the latter can be harder to pass up (hello, almighty dollar!). Say yes to new clients, part-ners, and social outings with careful thought and deliberation. If something doesn't feel like a good fit, don't invest too much energy in it. Seek out those who value and energize you. Your storage will thank you for it.

Don't wait until your metaphorical inbox is full because those hard stops can hurt in a lot of ways. Free up some space to keep things humming.

Summer Shandy

I slept with Nick on our third date. Well, technically, the morning after our third date. Twice.

The dentist I had gone out with a few times wouldn't ever have more than a beer. Which is fine. Except that I wasn't sure he knew how to cut loose.

Nick, on the other hand, picked me up for our third date in a cab. *Hell yes.*

He was wearing a blue and white checkered button-down that made his ocean eyes dance. Gosh, was he handsome. We settled into a tiny table at Basi Italia, which might be Columbus's most intimate restaurant, and enjoyed a bottle of wine with dinner. His hands were strong and masculine, I noticed, but also clean. He had grown up in Minnesota as the protective older brother of a sister with severe special needs, and he had a well of patience and empathy that was almost palpable. I didn't yet know just how much good stuff was beneath those soulful eyes. I just knew that he felt warm and real and easy.

After dinner, we went downtown to watch the Columbus Clippers play baseball and drank all the Leinenkugel Summer

Shandy in the stadium. (This is hardly an exaggeration. Nick was splitting season tickets with some friends, who went to a game the next day and sent him a photo of lemon wedges littered beneath the seats. "Dude," one of them texted. "What happened last night?") Nick kissed me at the ballpark. And then, drunk on summer romance and half the alcohol in the city, we fell asleep in my condo with music blaring so loud my neighbors later told me they could hear it half a block away as they rounded a corner to walk home.

We woke up with moderate hangovers and made love for the first time before we left the bed—a bold move, I might add, with a bloated belly. It was about as good as it gets for being as dehydrated as we were.

Nick was dog-sitting for a friend, so we threw on clothes, and I drove Nick to his place to let out the dog. He made us smoothies in his kitchen, which I complimented and learned he designed himself.

Is this guy for real?

We made our way up to his bedroom and had sex again. This time, fireworks.

Afterward, I went to the bathroom, took a breath, walked out, and looked at Nick. Was I about to fuck it all up?

"My last serious relationship," I said, slowly, "was with a woman."

Nick, naked and tan within a jumble of sheets, started laughing nervously.

"Why are you telling me this?" he asked.

"Because I want to be honest," I said. "About everything."

"Great," he said and then smiled. "But I don't care if you were with a woman."

My entire body exhaled.

I knew I wasn't going on any more dates with the dentist.

A week or two later, I was throwing my annual Keg Party Bonanza—a Memorial Day weekend party to welcome summer. KPB was held in my condo's tiny backyard. There were four kegs, twinkly lights, beer pong, flip cup, and pizza from my favorite neighborhood food truck. My neighbors gave Nick an earful about how KPB could make or break our new relationship. If he wanted to be my Summer Shandy, I said, he'd need to be the party's most fun guest—and its last man standing.

As my final friends filtered out that night and I stacked the red Solo cups, I found Nick on my living room couch, taking a snooze. I shook him awake.

"I'm the last one here," he said. "I guess I'm your Summer Shandy." And he was.

Of course, being the painfully honest girlfriend was easier in theory than in practice.

At the time, I was working at camp. It felt like the startup it was. We were building, creating, writing, eventing, raising money, putting on our stiletto heels, and then peeling them off to take out the trash. I was pouring myself into it, and I loved the mission and the work. But I was doing it for half of what I was used to living on. And I had burned through my savings after quitting my last job. However, I don't like to be taken care of, so I paid for as many dates as Nick would allow. (Truth be told, that wasn't many. "What would my grandfather think?" he said when I got out my card on that first date.) Regardless, my disposable income was almost nonexistent, and the expenses were adding up.

A year into dating, Nick said he wanted to take me on a trip to St. John. His treat. The idea of him buying a vacation felt uncomfortable, but I knew by then that I loved him—I loved every second of being with him—and I wanted to go. So I said yes.

When we arrived, I wanted to contribute by buying our groceries.

But holy shit, groceries in St. John's are expensive. We wanted tequila and club soda, and as we stood in shorts and sandals in the aisle of that steamy grocery store, I found two club soda options— one twenty dollars more than the other. I grabbed the cheaper version.

"This other brand is really good," Nick said. "Let's just get it."

It sparked an enormous fight—all because I didn't tell him what I needed, which was, in that moment, to contribute in a way that I could afford to.

Later that year, at our favorite café one night, I started crying.

"I'm tired. I'm working seven days a week," I said. "I can barely pay my bills. I'm stressed about money all the time."

He was mortified. How had he missed that? He felt terrible I was carrying that burden.

Shortly after, he surprised me with a generous donation to my nonprofit.

(The move prompted what is unequivocally the most hilarious directive I have ever gotten or will get from a boss. After Nick's check arrived, the CEO walked into my office to share the news. "I hope you give him a blow job," she said. She would eventually officiate our wedding.)

As an important aside, I also finally asked for what I needed at that nonprofit: a raise. I scheduled time with the CEO, made a very strong case for what I had brought to the table—including tens of thousands of dollars saved because I was constantly leveraging creative contacts to offer high-level work at a discount—and shared metrics that most marketing directors were making twice my salary. Two weeks later, my salary nearly doubled. All because I asked.

But back to Nick.

I wish I could say it only took that one lapse to learn my lesson about communicating my needs. It did not.

Dorothy, our first child, was born on January 8, when it was six degrees below zero. Which means the ensuing days in my charming, walkable 'hood weren't exactly warm. Read: I was trapped. My sweet mother was making her best effort to help, bringing daily piles of spaghetti and meatballs (helpful to Nick but not a nursing mother) and once unloading a dishwasher filled with what she thought were clean dishes (she was wrong). Then my in-laws flew in to join the fray. Seven days in, I needed maxi pads and was dying for a fresh-squeezed juice. Dorothy was asleep, so I looked for all of my helpers. Nick was asleep. As was his dad. And his mom.

So I bundled up and set out for CVS and the organic juice café. I had just given birth. I was exhausted. And I was pissed. But shame on me. I chose to play the martyr instead of asking for what I needed. I realized once again that, as much as I anticipate the needs of others, I can't expect them to anticipate mine. Even one week postpartum.

The good news: I had gotten better by daughter number two. A few months after Maeve was born, I told Nick I needed time away. Alone.

I recognize that many men would have either balked ("No, I'm not staying home for a weekend with an infant and a toddler"), or judged ("What kind of mother are you?"), or felt threatened ("You don't want to get away together?").

"Where do you want to go?" Nick asked. He then promptly used his travel points to put me in Chicago's swankiest hotel.

Thankfully, you see, I didn't marry any of those other men. I married my Summer Shandy.

BUCKET-FILLERS: KNOW THEM. BE THEM. RAISE THEM.

One sunny afternoon, I was watching my daughter Dorothy, who was two, play with a neighbor outside.

The boy climbed up onto a little wall we have on our patio and raced back and forth. Dorothy observed him with admiration and tried to do the same.

"You can't do it, Dorothy!" I heard him say to her as she gripped the edge.

She struggled, and he doubled down.

"I told you, you couldn't do it!"

After explaining to her friend that we don't speak to each other like that in our house, I assured Dorothy that she could, in fact, do it.

She tried again and reached the top.

We all have that little boy in our lives, don't we? Someone who, for whatever reason, fills us with doubt and uncertainty. These are bucket-spillers.

Bucket-fillers, however, do the opposite. With genuine words of encouragement, they fill us with confidence and energy. We're suddenly able to accomplish goals we never thought possible. We become strong, capable, and self-assured. For this reason, I keep a steadfast group of bucket-fillers in my life.

This didn't come easy, however. I've spent many years intentionally trying to surround myself with voices of positivity. Here's how I did it.

Set boundaries with bucket-spillers.
If we're being honest with ourselves, we know it's not always possible to phase out *all* of our bucket-spillers. So we have to identify what makes us feel successful in our interactions with them, and then set boundaries to achieve that.

Whenever I feel depleted and unbalanced, I know my bucket's been spilled. So I survey how I've spent my time, and I set boundaries with the bucket-spillers in my life to make sure I fill back up.

Seek out bucket-fillers (even when it's not convenient).
You may have to sacrifice convenience to be around your bucket-fillers, but you likely won't regret that.

I relish Orangetheory, a fitness program that leaves me feeling exhausted and accomplished after each workout. One of the coaches at my studio is particularly motivating—I've successfully blasted my rowing goals with his help—so I seek him out whenever I'm there. It's not always convenient, but it is always worth it.

You know who your bucket-fillers are. Make sure they're a consistent part of your life, whether it means scheduling a lunch once a month or simply making a point to drop by the right person's desk more often.

Fill others' buckets—and accept having yours filled, too.
If you aren't a bucket-filler, you're likely a spiller. So be supportive and encouraging in your relationships to perpetuate positivity. Identify when others might need their buckets filled and be intentional about filling them. Bonus points: when someone is trying to fill your bucket, accept their generosity.

One day, I ran into a woman who lives in my neighborhood, and, much to my surprise, she had an infant strapped to her body. We aren't close enough for me to have known she'd had a second child. I asked how she was doing, remembering all too well what it was like to juggle two during those early weeks.

"It's been a challenge," she said.

I first asked her how I could help, and she didn't have an answer. Then, I offered something tangible: "Bring your three-year-old to my house to play for an afternoon, and you can snuggle your newborn uninterrupted." She said yes. I was so impressed by her ability to accept help when it was offered. Because let's be honest: many of us struggle to accept help, believing we're supposed to be able to do it all. My friends, my hope is that when life feels overwhelming, you will have the courage to say yes when someone sincerely wants to support you.

Whether you're a spiller, a filler, or someone accepting the fill with gratitude, know that whoever is watching you—your kids, your partner, your coworkers—will take note.

As Dorothy gripped the wall that sunny afternoon, I knew all she needed was a few cheerful words from a bucket-filler. Once she got them, she reached her goal.

The bonus? Filling others' buckets, in turn, fills our own.

Fill on.

The Invisible Load

"Mommy, my belly hurts."

What we say: "I'm so sorry, sweetheart. Let's get you some water, get into your jammies, and go to bed a little early. It'll be fine by morning."

What we think: *Shit. If she's running a fever by tomorrow, daycare won't take her. I can't miss my keynote, and Nick's out of town. Mom can't help because she has two doctors' appointments. Maybe Julie's sitter can come. If she can, Maeve will be sobbing as I walk out the door because I'm leaving her with someone she's only met once. Still, a win. Wait—what do I look like as I walk out the door? Did the cleaners drop everything off today? I need my red blazer for tomorrow, and Nick needs his navy suit for Friday night. Are those dry-cleaning chemicals slowly killing us? I need to try that new organic moisturizer Liz was talking about. Oh my gosh, Liz's birthday is Monday and I still haven't grabbed a gift. I'll do it Saturday after yoga. I swear, when I turned forty, my body stopped burning fat. WTF. Maybe I should get back into Muay Thai. Just saw on Facebook that the woman I used to train with is in London. Why do I keep putting off that trip? I'll look at airfare tonight. Maybe we should live abroad. We could totally down-size and do the apartment thing. The new buyers are going to love our kitchen reno. But should I have gone with the darker hardwood?*

Ah, the invisible load. It's what most of us carry, day in and day out. We handle the bulk of the parenting duties. Schedule medical appointments. Deal with insurance matters. Plan holiday gatherings. Pay bills. Nurture friendships. Book vacations.

Sure, it means the lives of everyone around us run smoothly. The girls end up at gymnastics on time, the right jersey is clean for game day, a new gallon of milk hits the fridge before the old one runs out, the summer beach house is secured twelve months in advance, Christmas gifts appear beneath the tree (even for us!), and the rummy score is properly kept.

But constantly anticipating others' needs also weighs us down, sometimes in ways we don't even recognize.

One emotion I often see in clients and friends is something most of us don't want to talk about: we feel underwhelmed. We've climbed to the top of the mountain we thought we wanted to be on, and when we get there, it's not what we envisioned.

Sometimes, marriage becomes the scapegoat. I have a client who started exploring the idea of divorcing her husband. She was looking at apartments. She met with a co-parenting counselor.

"It's important that your kids know that your love for them isn't broken," the counselor said. "It's the marriage that's broken."

My client had a total epiphany. She and her husband, she realized, weren't broken at all. It was the weight of the invisible load that had broken her. She wanted to break up with her life. And now, she's taking positive steps to do that—to redefine what she wants and to understand how to get it.

The first step, then? Recognizing your invisible load. Like most challenges in life, identifying its existence is half the battle. And I'll be the first to admit, I am far from perfect. But I've gotten better at recognizing the load I carry so that I can unpack it a piece at a time.

Take, for example, the holidays. I buy all of the gifts, including my own, and then wrap them and tuck them neatly beneath the tree. I also buy the girls' gifts from my mom. I preorder the cinnamon rolls that have become a Christmas morning tradition and pick them up on Christmas Eve. I simultaneously buy Dorothy's birthday presents. I order her cake as soon as the new year hits. I pick up (and then promptly hide) helium balloons on January 7. And in the wee hours of January 8—her big day—I tie balloons to each of the dining room chairs downstairs, where her perfectly wrapped gifts await. I schedule time during the day to pick up her cake and get home early to set up our little party. And in the midst of it all, I also find ways to celebrate our nanny, whose birthday is on the exact same day (of course!).

There are moments I wonder whether Nick notices what it takes to pull it off. And when the hell he's going to offer to help. So this year, I did what I would coach any of my clients to do: I found one easy way he could contribute and asked for what I needed. He picked up my mother, who can no longer drive, so she could enjoy the party with us, and then drove her home afterward. Gladly, might I add. And thanked me for always pulling everything together. (I'm already plotting what else I can add to his list next year.)

Speaking of birthdays, if your crew is delivering you a stellar one every year, good for you. This year, mine looked like this: Maeve woke me up at 5:15 a.m., having wet the bed. I tried getting her back to sleep to no avail, so I just got up with her. By 6:15, I was microwaving frozen pancakes while making French toast, washing Maeve's urine-soaked sheets, and unloading the dishwasher. Nick sauntered down around 7:30 or 8, and it was probably half an hour before it hit him. "Happy birthday," he finally said. As hard as I work to make everyone else's birthdays stellar, I don't care much about mine. So this is honestly fine for me. But I share it to say that I know what you other mommas are living through. And if you're big birthday peeps, this might be killing you slowly, or at the very least building bitterness. So here's my suggestion: give your partner a wish list. Ask your kiddos to make you cards. And throw your own damn party.

Another piece many of us neglect is our health. I'm vigilant about certain things—dental cleanings, mammograms, dermatologist checkups. But I occasionally find myself in the same bad health habit trap I coach so many women out of: deprioritizing workouts. Which is detrimental to my mental health. I recalibrate and recommit. I remind myself it's not a guilty pleasure; it's a necessity for my well-being and, therefore, the well-being of my family. Nobody gets anywhere on an empty tank. So, ladies, ask for the time you need from your partner and from yourself. And then protect it like you mean it.

If you don't—and I'll wager a bet you have a story similar to this one—here is what happens.

One morning, shortly after I had Dorothy, I was drowning in new parenthood. Three new mom friends came over for coffee and a chat. Nick was home, so I had signed up for yoga at noon. I told the group how excited I was. Two of the three mommas left by 11:15. The third somehow missed both the memo and the social cues. She talked, and talked, and talked.

11:34 a.m. *I have to go*, I said silently. My leg started to shake nervously.

Then my friend's baby needed to be changed. So she undressed the babe and started removing the diaper. Slowly. So, so slowly. She stopped mid-change to make a dramatic point in her story. I wasn't paying attention to a word she said.

11:42 a.m. *OK*, I thought, *I can't walk to yoga now. I'll just drive.*

She continued changing the diaper. Telling her story. Completely oblivious to my absolute panic. All I wanted was yoga. But I didn't want to hurt her feelings.

11:51 a.m. *Holy fuck*, I thought. *I'm not going to get to class.*

She finally walked out at 11:58. I shut the door behind her and cried. Pissed I was missing yoga. Pissed at her. Pissed at myself.

I should have just said, "Kate, you have to be gone by 11:30." Or, "I have to leave, so you're free to change the diaper and then let yourself out." But I didn't. Because that hour, on that morning, the invisible load—it's your responsibility to manage everyone else's feelings!—crushed me.

The truth is, ladies, many of us struggle with that invisible load. It's how we're wired. But brick by brick, we can deconstruct it. We can lighten our loads. And can we live more freely.

What is it that you need today?

CREATE SPACE TO TRANSFORM
(BEFORE LIFE DOES IT FOR YOU)

My friend had been talking about leaving her lackluster and high-stress job for over ten years. It seemed she always had one more project to see through, though—until her position was eliminated. "That was the best gift I've ever received," she told me. She's happier, she said, and her marriage is thriving like never before.

Another client who also disliked her job told me she's always had an age in mind for when she'll quit. But a recent health scare is making her reconsider putting it off.

Stories like these make me wonder: *why do we so often wait for the other shoe to drop before we take action?*

It's frighteningly easy to fill your time with work and obligations that bring you minimal or no joy. **But if you're after meaningful transformation, you have to make space for it to happen.**

That means taking steps to ensure you have time and energy to put toward whatever it is you want. Here are three space-making strategies.

Rewrite the rules. What is one thing you wish you could do (or stop doing) that you think is impossible? Write it down—and then flip the script. What looks different when you challenge the notion that it can't happen? If you'd like to quit your job, perhaps you realize it is possible if you're willing to shift your budget. Play out an alternative storyline and see how you feel.

Take predictable time off. I love this idea drawn from a *Harvard Business Review* study. It suggests identifying a block of time each week to unplug from work entirely—as in, leaving the office and committing to not checking email or voicemail. The study clearly states the benefits of predictable time off (participants felt refreshed, and their work showed it, among other things). Sometimes if we want space, we have to schedule it for ourselves.

Chip away at the unessential. Try Greg McKeown's 90 percent rule (which I mention a couple of times in this book because it is gold). Which obligations, commitments, and invitations would you rank below 90 percent on your scale of personal fulfillment? Get rid of what you can. Outsource, delegate, or decline. The more you do it, the more space you'll have for the remaining 10 percent that lights you up.

Don't wait for life to create the space you already know you need. Make it yourself.

Bag of Urine

Sometimes, the loads we carry are, in fact, visible. Case in point: I once had an ongoing pants-wetting problem.

My doctors were working really hard to fix it. At that point in my life, being published in *Harvard Business Review* was my nearly singular professional mission. I could envision receiving the news that it was finally happening: I would be sitting in my sweet office digs, overlooking our bustling arts district, probably popping open a bottle of Veuve Clicquot as I prepared for one of my intimate mom-boss seminars.

Know when I got the call? As I sat in a parking lot with a catheter, its garden-hose-sized tube running beneath my maxi dress and a bag of urine hidden in a reusable grocery bag.

But of course.

Here's to the loads we carry, ladies—invisible or otherwise. Cheers.

Grab the Grapefruit

I found a note that my mother wrote to her mother on February 15, 1968. At that point, my parents had three kids—Ann, Pat, and Peter—and Mom was pregnant with a baby she would eventually lose. Long-distance calls were, at that time, too expensive to regularly make. So letters it was. And this one, which so beautifully illustrates a mother's struggle, is solid gold.

Dear Mom,

What a week I've had—spelled P-E-T-E-R. Brother. Who'd have him but a mother?

Kent (neighbor kid) and Pat have a two-foot hole dug in the sandbox. Wednesday, Peter got stuck in it—up to his knees in mud. I had to get Karen (Kent's mom) to help me pull him free. What a mess! Snowsuit—boots—me—mud! That p.m. he took a cover off of Ann's foam rubber pillow and shredded it all over. I just cried and left it until Leo got home at 11 p.m. to help me shake bedding, etc. Ann slept in my room.

Peter then flooded the bathroom while I made fudge Thursday. Rug—floor—to basement went H2o. That a.m. he cut several pages out of a hardcover book I borrowed from Elanor—so that I have to replace! He got cover off and dumped

nose drops on both Leo's and my beds, etc. He weakens me. I
let him deliver Valentines yesterday. He came home with an ice
cream cone from the two women across the street. They love him,
anyway.
      Well—hair's combed out. Off to shop.

Love, Jan.

Years later, by the time she had all six of her kiddos, Mom used to
grab a grapefruit from the kitchen, lock herself in the bathroom, sit
on the toilet, and savor her favorite fruit.

"The idea of cutting up grapefruit for six of you felt exhausting,"
she once told me. "So I just ate it alone."

It's so relatable, right?

I love this vision because it perfectly illustrates the cold, hard
realities of parenting—the exhaustion, the chaos, and the desperate
desire for a moment of peace, even if it comes on the toilet. But I
also love it because she knew what she needed, and she showed up
for herself.

Another favorite story is the one Mom tells about my first day of
kindergarten. She was, at the time, a full-time mom, and I was the
youngest of six. She watched me walk out the door, turned around,
promptly laid down on the couch, and took a nap.

Raise your hands, ladies. Ask the question. Claim your space. Find
your moment. You're everyone else's superhero; be your own, too.

CHAPTER FIVE

Front Porch Wieners

{Give Yourself a Break}

"A person who never made a mistake
never tried anything new."

—Albert Einstein

ront Porch Wieners, an annual party I throw on July 4, is
basically a sophisticated kegger.

The first year I hosted it, I was single, living in my condo,
and looking for a way to make my favorite day of the year even better. So I invited bunches of people to my place on the fourth when
Columbus's colorful Doo Dah parade makes its way through my
neighborhood. I asked each guest to share his or her favorite hot
dog order in advance. Then, I created a menu listing each guest's
signature dog.

Regan: relish, onion, celery salt, and mustard.

I had a professional designer friend create the (beautiful) menus
and posters, too. I orchestrated help from others to offer what

would have been an Instagram-worthy party if social media had existed then: intricately decorated cupcakes that I displayed on a tray with sparklers; chocolate-dipped pretzels with red, white, and blue sprinkles; and miniature Oscar Mayer Wienermobile Hot Wheels in honor of my brother Mike's gig as a Hotdogger.

The inaugural party was epic.

By 2018, with two girls under three and not enough hours in any given week, our July 4 guests walked up our path to this: Nick grilling dogs on the porch beside a keg, bags of help-yourself buns, and a giant tub of cheese balls. (Cheese balls—you know, the kind you see in Sam's Club that look kind of fun but that nobody actually buys or eats? Yep, those.) So not exactly sophisticated. But you know what? Front Porch Wieners is alive and well.

This, friends, is among my keys to joy: give yourself a break. Let it go. Or, as another mom-boss girlfriend and I often say—an homage we challenge ourselves to take literally—sign up for the plates and napkins. (Every mom in America knows exactly what I'm talking about. Because most of you have, at some point, been at up 1 a.m. slaving over Pinterest-perfect cupcakes you signed up to take to the class party, despising that little part of you that finds it important to impress five-year-olds, or their teacher, or whoever the hell it is you thought you were trying to impress on first-day-of-school party sign-ups.)

You can't do it all. Neither can I. Instead, I've learned to give myself a break. Front Porch Wieners, for example, might no longer suggest I was, at one point, a professional event planner. Who cares? My people come, and we enjoy each other. That's the whole point anyway.

Of course, I'm always learning. Take, for example, my youngest daughter's baby book.

I usually make vacation goals. On one trip, one of those goals was to start Maeve's baby book. She was turning three. THREE. While I have little mom guilt, the fact that there weren't photos of her in a book is something I definitely felt bad about, but with reason. This kiddo looked at the one family album that we had, which is all about her big sister's first year, on repeat. She pointed to the photos, thinking they were of her. I stopped correcting her because it felt easier than breaking her little heart.

Despite the fact I coach people not to do this (sigh), I kept putting off making hers because I knew it would take me too long to get it just right. So on vacation, after a few poolside beers, I finally logged onto Shutterfly and opted to have them design the book for me. It took about twenty minutes to upload the photos. And suddenly, I had a baby book. Bam.

Is it 100 percent my style? No. But the pictures are of Maeve, and that was the primary requirement. I gave Maeve a sneak peek, and she was over the moon. When we returned from vacation and UPS delivered a package that wasn't her book, Maeve's look of disappointment hurt my heart. She asked a dozen times when it was coming until it finally arrived.

Was it perfect for me? Nope. Was it perfect for Maeve? Absolutely. Because it was done.

Women, as we've discussed, carry a particularly heavy invisible load. We air traffic control our families like experts, coordinating daycare, packing lunches, washing laundry, communicating with teachers, and scheduling doctor's appointments. We do it at work, too, mentoring colleagues, mothering interns, offering nutrition advice to the woman who wants to start somewhere, sharing books to read, and reminding HR that there really should be tampons in the ladies' room. We carry the invisible load of creating plans B, C, D, and E on any given day.

I've come a long way in shifting my mindset when my plans (or dreams) take an unexpected turn.

One morning, for example, my childcare fell through. I was forced to cancel plans, reschedule meetings, and pause a project I was super eager to get my hands on. Four years ago, I would have blown a gasket. This time, I said, "Oh well." I asked a major favor of someone so I could make the most essential meeting of my day. And I then made an airplane out of a cardboard box with my kids and had an impromptu birthday party for someone I know, all before 8 a.m.

You can't always choose what comes your way, but you can always choose how you show up for yourself in that moment.

Of course, we don't always get that critical meeting in. Or we don't get the baby book done. Or we don't host the party at all. Or we forget it was pajama day at school. Or we don't close the deal. Or finish the marathon. Or save the marriage. Guess what? *That's okay, too.*

Sometimes, good enough is good enough. Other times, failing epically is in order. We'll feel embarrassed, even humiliated. But give yourself a break. Let go of the shit weighing you down. Forgive yourself. Forgive others. Move forward.

We are, after all, human. And we're all in this together.

TAKING BIG SHOTS (AND THE UPSIDE OF MISSING)

My dad played for Naperville High School's basketball team. They were in the state finals. He had the opportunity to make a game-winning shot. As a man with deep faith, he made a promise to God: if I make this shot, I'll become a priest.

Thank the Lord he missed.

What my dad couldn't have realized at that time is that he was destined to have a much different legacy. He would marry a stunner of a redhead, raise six children with her, leave the stability of a corporate job to start a successful family business, and so much more.

The moral? Missing the shot—while devastating at the time—can turn into the best gift of all.

Take, for example, the rejection letter I got from Miami University— the university all five of my older siblings attended. While humiliating, it was a gift I didn't know I needed. Attending Ohio University allowed me a different college experience than my siblings—one that led to an internship on Capitol Hill, a semester abroad, connections that landed me my first job in Manhattan (which in turn led me to world travel) and, twenty years later, the closest friendships a girl could dream up. The lesson? That rejection letter was life redirecting me to the right path.

Being laid off during the recession of 2008 paved the way for reflecting on what I really wanted to do with my next chapter: work for the greater good. What an honor to have been able to say yes to being the Chief Storyteller at Flying Horse Farms, a camp for children with serious illnesses that hadn't yet opened. Helping get camp up off the ground is one of my proudest accomplishments. The upside to losing my job? Finding what was, at the time, my calling—which eventually led me to this one.

A few years back, I got a group email from Marshall Goldsmith, who is ranked as the number one executive coach in the world. His work has influenced me personally and professionally. And when people play that game of "If you could have dinner with any living person, who would it be?" he's at the top of my list. So this email said Goldsmith was launching a program called 15 Coaches. He planned to choose and teach fifteen coaches everything he knows. For free. The only "fee" was that the fifteen people had to pay it forward to fifteen others (for free) when the time was right. I applied. And not only did I apply, but I also told my entire audience—from clients to casual followers—that I was taking that leap. It was scary posting my dream for everyone to read. Sure, over 8,000 people had applied, but I felt in my core that the opportunity was destined for me.

"Is this lofty? Yes." I wrote at the time. "But I'll take lofty over regret any day."

When I was rejected, then, the blow was that much worse. Instead of wallowing in my sorrow, though, I bounced forward and actively reached out to people I wanted to learn from. The effort led me to Denise Restauri, who featured me in *Forbes* and opened doors for me to become a contributor myself. Best of all, that mentorship evolved into a friendship that I now cherish. My takeaway, once again? Expect to love the unexpected gifts rejection has in store— they are better than anything you could dream up.

Of course, here's the rub: to miss shots, you must first take them. Here, then, is to taking big shots—wherever they end up.

Colleen

My first real boss was the grossest. He was a schmoozer—a guy who would do the finger gun with a click-click when he walked by. I was a fresh college grad working for a big-deal communications firm in New York, and he didn't train me, let alone coach me. I was supposed to cold call, win, and then nurture potential clients. He said, "Circle back," to me on repeat without offering guidance on what to do between the comment and the circling back. Despite him—flying by the seat of my pants without any support but full of gumption and spunk—I had managed to grow a new lead into a half-million-dollar account.

By the grace of God, Colleen noticed.

I first met Colleen when I went to New York as part of a corporate leaders program at Ohio University. Another OU alum worked at her firm, so we visited. They asked who was interested in an impromptu interview, and I raised my hand. A few of us were ushered into Colleen's office. It was 4:30 p.m. on a cold, rainy Friday afternoon, and despite the fact I recognized that talking to some Midwestern college kids instead of starting her weekend was probably the last thing Colleen wanted to be doing, she was friendly and interested. Super easy to talk to. I was so impressed by her. Plus, she had a giant jar of candy in her office, which I loved. I got the job.

A few months later, I was sitting on the top floor of a beautiful Manhattan building, having lunch with Colleen. She was pulling me from the receiving end of Mr. Schmoozer's finger guns and into her candy jar sphere. I would report directly to her, she explained, helping plan and execute executive events around the world.

Colleen became my boss, my mentor, my teacher, and my friend.

We worked for the events arm of the firm. She provided structure, scheduling weekly check-ins. And she allowed me a front-row seat to watch her work. She quickly started taking me on trips I didn't need to be on simply to let me learn—and giving up her personal privacy to let me bunk with her, so I didn't become an added expense.

Our events, mainly for tech company sales teams, were really something spectacular. Of course, because we were producing live events, there was constant chaos. We always needed one last thing. I once found myself running the streets of Dubai, desperately searching for a walking stick we needed as the trophy for a Yoda award we were giving. (I found it. Along with the gold foil-wrapped chocolate coins we needed, too.)

But despite the pressure that could have suffocated anyone, Colleen carefully balanced our stress with fun. In Dubai, we rode camels and went sand surfing. In Bali, we white water rafted. In Singapore, we got drunk on Singapore Slings.

She taught me how to ask for help. (Do it early and directly.) She once pulled me into her office and made a call on speakerphone to teach me how to deliver disappointing news. (Be honest, accept responsibility, apologize and mean it, and share the game plan for forward progress.) And she developed my business muscles by trusting me even before I thought I was ready. (She once sent me alone to Hawaii with a longtime client she had nurtured for years.)

She also offered a master class in making others feel special. She decorated my cube on my birthday. She treated me to burgers and fries at New York's finest joints—Pastis in the Meatpacking District, JG Melon on the Upper East Side. She shared years' worth of hard-earned city secrets—best place for a cream puff, best place for a black and white cookie. She generously shared tickets and seats (box ones, often; she's always had all the connections): Yankees games, Mets games, Neil Diamond at Madison Square Garden, the US Open Tennis Championships.

She hosted amazing parties. On my first St. Patrick's Day in New York, my roommate and I woke up early, started drinking, hit the *Today Show* plaza, and then watched the parade on Fifth Avenue before the main event: Colleen's legendary St. Patty's Day soiree. Her place was just a few blocks off the route, filled with corned beef, cabbage, cake from the city's finest bakery, and one hell of a guest list. She even invited me to dinner with her parents so often that they eventually gifted me the same red plate they had gifted Colleen and her brother, which says, "You are special today."

And she gave the most thoughtful presents. I have a beautiful Waterford shamrock she gifted me on one occasion and a Tiffany key ring from her that I use to this day.

Because of Colleen, I pay attention to details. I remember birthdays. I pick up the tab for younger people. I give people chances they probably don't deserve. I gift thoughtfully. I can throw a killer party (Front Porch Wieners will someday resurrect in all its glory, I'm sure). And I know that when I have to deliver disappointing news—to others or myself—that I can do it with grace, chase it with a Singapore Sling, let that shit go, and forge ahead.

LISTEN BETTER AND MULTITASK WORSE

You're in the middle of typing an email when a colleague walks in with a question. You look up, fingers still flying across your keyboard, and answer. You may or may not know what she asked.

You bring your laptop to a meeting, hoping to work double-duty, marking off to-dos as others talk. You haven't a clue what was decided in the meeting.

You pull out your phone during each stop in play at your daughter's soccer game, making good use of every possible moment. And you later swear you absolutely saw her score the goal you actually missed.

Multitasking is often hailed as a useful skill. After all, we figure tackling multiple chores at once results in higher productivity, getting us closer and closer to that next benchmark. But what happens when multitasking takes the place of listening?

Back when I was less aware of how multitasking was affecting my relationships, I prided myself on typing and talking all at once. (I don't even need to look at my keyboard!) What was I telling the colleague in front of me about what I valued? I'd also greet my husband as he walked through the door without putting down my phone. "How was your day?" I'd ask, half-listening for an answer. What was I telling him about how much I cared? I felt efficient. He likely felt jilted.

Chances are, if we're doing two things at the same time, we're doing one of them poorly. I've worked in a lot of environments (creative ones, especially) that celebrate the art of multitasking at the cost of human connection, and it always ended in half-baked work and relationships. The latter bothers me more.

On my quest to be more present, I made a point to close my laptop and put down my phone if a human being was in front of me. The results were palpable: more meaningful conversations, clarity around my work, fewer meetings to discuss previous meetings.

But if you feel that for you, it's not that simple, here are a few tricks to being a better listener—and a worse multitasker:

1. **Capture three facts during a conversation to replay.**
   If you're talking with a colleague, try to find small bits of information you can return to later. What if you remembered that they were visiting a relative in poor health this weekend and asked them about it on Monday? What if you knew they were nervous about an upcoming presentation and made sure to check in after it ended? My friend Colleen set the gold standard on this and, in doing so, taught me that listening and caring at this level of depth makes for relationships that are satisfying and fruit-bearing.

2. **Dig deeper.** Start small by asking one follow-up question in every conversation you have today. It shows you are listening and that you are interested.

3. **Designate a space for your device.** My brother's family has a no-phones-in-the-kitchen rule. The kitchen is for communing, and there's no place for multitasking at the table. If you find yourself in bed, phone in hand,

wasting precious time with your spouse as you scan social media, find a plug across the room and leave your phone there to charge.

Multitasking doesn't need to come at the cost of our presence. Show up for people and yourself.

♥

9/11

I was out of foundation and lipstick. So I decided to pop into the most convenient Sephora heading into work. I walked into the makeup mecca on the ground floor of the illustrious Twin Towers, grabbed what I needed, and checked out.

It was September 10, 2001.

The next morning, I took the train from Hoboken to Fourteenth Street and walked beneath the warm, late-summer sun into the Chelsea Market building. What had once been the original Nabisco factory had evolved into a popular market filled with unique boutiques peddling goodies from cupcakes to flowers. It was colorful and vibrant, teeming with the New York energy I loved. A handful of the city's most creative companies called the exposed-brick spaces above the market home. Including mine.

It was early, still, as I walked into our office. I poured myself a cup of coffee, emailed a few friends—remember a time when we didn't text everything?—and started prepping for our next wave of events.

"A plane just hit the Trade Center tower," someone said.

Wait. What?

It was 8:46 a.m. I didn't know who said it. But Pennie, the president of our division, had a TV in her office, so we headed in. We turned on The Today Show, watching silently, not so much terrified—because we didn't yet know we should be—as we were shocked.

Soon, leadership pulled everyone together.

"We think people should stay put," they said. "But do what you want."

Because no one knew.

Then the second plane hit the other tower.

And life as we knew it changed for good.

Trains stopped running. The National Guard began lining the streets. My friend Jamie, who also worked in Manhattan but lived in Hoboken, met me at the market so we could walk to the ferry to get home.

We walked through streets that were silent aside from the chorus of sirens. No one talked. People who had been near Ground Zero walked past us, covered in ashes. The Red Cross had hastily assembled a blood donation center in Hoboken, we learned. We'd go directly there, we agreed. But as we rode across the water, we realized there was no need to give blood. No one had survived.

So we walked to my apartment and met two other friends. We ordered pizza. Watched the news. Worried about whether people we knew were alive. My phone rang incessantly with people back home, including my high school sweetheart, calling to make sure I was okay. I tried desperately to reach Greg, a trader I had dated. The phone lines were clogged. I tried and tried, growing more desperate each time I dialed before I finally got through. He had survived but witnessed atrocities—like people jumping from windows—that nobody should. I was relieved he was alive. We haven't spoken since.

That evening, we walked to a park for a candlelight vigil and prayed. Across the Hudson River, we could still see smoke rising from where the towers that morning had stood. Afterward, we sat at a local bar and talked over beers. There was something important about being around people, about staying together.

Three weeks later, every phone pole and pillar in the city was still plastered with people's pictures and names. *Have you seen Joe?* I went to pick up my dry cleaning, and the owner's eyes softened when I walked in.

"I'm so happy to see your face," she said.

I wonder how many items she cleaned were never picked up.

In October, our division president, Pennie, called Colleen, me, and a few others into the same office where we'd watched the world unravel. The stock market had tanked. Our biggest client lost everything. We no longer had jobs.

We weren't surprised. Still, it was another blow—the abrupt end of a damn good chapter.

But we were alive to fight another day. And in New York, in the fall of 2001, that made us very, very lucky.

When I got my credit card statement later that month, I looked at my Sephora purchase from September 10.

8:52 a.m.

I suppose sometimes, for whatever reason, the universe gives you a break. And that, I know, was a miraculous one.

PLATES & NAPKINS: THE MOM-BOSS POWER PLAY

My friend looked at her second-grade son's classroom party sign-up sheet.

- *Healthy snacks*
- *Sweet treats*
- *Drinks*
- *Crafts/games*
- *Plates & napkins*

Everybody likes the sweet treats best. That's why she's always signed up for them.

But she's a CEO with an especially full and exciting plate at work, evenings packed with soccer games she doesn't want to miss, a marriage she's working to nurture, sleep she's finally started getting, and the same twenty-four hours a day as the rest of us.

She circled "plates & napkins" and texted me a photo.

Bam.

She shed the should of proving to that second-grade classroom she's boss. Why? Because she knows she's boss. She'd mapped out her priorities and knew that by saying yes to cupcakes, she would have been saying no to precious late-night alone time with her husband or much-needed sleep. And that, my friends, is a win. The power play has become part of our everyday vernacular now. Did you turn down the opportunity to sit on the board and instead just write a check? You plates-and-napkins'd it. Did you just order pizza for dinner instead of cooking your parents a meal that would have knocked their socks off? You plates-and-napkins'd that, too.

If you're reading this, it's probably in part because circling plates and napkins isn't in your nature.

But when we try to be all things to all people, we fail. And you know who we usually fail most epically? Ourselves.

I love this saying: *you can have anything you want; you just can't have everything you want.*

It's so true. Yet many of us still live like we can have it all. We can run the company, attend the soccer games, thrive in the marriage, get our beauty sleep, *and* make the godforsaken, Pinterest-perfect cupcakes. But at what cost?

I read a book in which the author writes about the stress she used to have preparing Christmas Eve dinner. Her kids never really appreciated the meal, and she missed out on the merriment because she was stuck in the kitchen. Her solution? She asked her kids what they'd really like for dinner. They wanted In-N-Out Burger. So now, that's what they eat for Christmas Eve—on fine china. She gets to enjoy the merriment, the kids love the food, and they still all sit around the family table for a meal that feels special.

How great is that? A lot of us feel super anxious around the holidays. I hear it over and over. So I'll ask you what I often ask clients during the holiday season: what might happen if you lower your expectations?

What would happen, for example, if you had a potluck instead of doing all the cooking yourself? What would happen if you bought a pie instead of baking one from scratch? What would happen if you skipped the ribbons on the gifts instead of slaving over hand-tied bows on each? What would happen if you ditched the extended-family-house-hopping and rented a giant cabin for your whole crew instead?

I, for example, RSVP "no" to what I lovingly call The Holiday Gong Show. I skip the professional family portrait (and often the card, too). I pick only a few select parties to attend. I double down on yoga classes. And I wake up early each morning to spend as much quiet time as possible gazing at my Christmas tree, appreciating what has been and what might be. Instead of leaving me depleted, then, as December has done in years past, it leaves me filled up and ready for a new year.

Giving up some control around the holidays—and life in general—could yield some big gains for you, too.

I mean, I know no other mom is going to lead the PTO like you do. But you've paid your dues. If you pass the presidential baton to the next mom, could you finally get to that weekly yoga class you can never seem to find time for? Could you organize the basement that's driven you mad for a decade? Or could you buy an hour a week to lay in your hammock with a beer and simply do nothing? (Because despite what we convince ourselves, there is no law that women have to be moving from the moment we wake until the moment our heads hit our pillows at night.)

It's easy to default to what always has been. You've always made the sweet treat. You've always been PTO president. You've always led the Girl Scout troop. You've always organized the baseball car pool. You've always hosted Christmas.

But next time you make a decision on something, before you default to what always has been, take a beat. How do you want to feel in that given situation or circumstance? Who do you want to be in the room? How do you want to engage with others? What memories do you want to walk away with?

Then, build from there.

Bottom line? Life can be complicated—sometimes at our own doing. Remember that you don't just control your own destiny, but you also control your anxiety level along the journey. Find your plates-and-napkins moment. Seize it. And enjoy the benefits.

Parenting: The Ultimate Test

Nothing forces you to let shit go like parenting.

As I write this chapter, I'm on vacation. In a beach mansion. With family, including my sister Ann, who is cooking gourmet dinners nightly. Want to know what I'm doing? Crying.

Because my girls do not adapt well to new environments. Or, quite frankly, people in general. So each morning here, as we walk to the breakfast table in this three-story beauty of a home overlooking the ocean, my siblings, nieces, and nephews say good morning. Dorothy responds with a growl. Literally. And it just gets worse from there—meanness, yelling, and tantrums escalate from zero to sixty in an eye blink. Maeve isn't much better.

"Girls," I implored this morning, "how would you feel if people treated you this way?"

I am beyond embarrassed; I'm seething. I'm second-guessing my parenting abilities. Am I not raising friendly kids? Or am I being overbearing and overcritical, trying to over-edit who they are? I have spent every second on edge. I honestly just want to go home.

Instead, I'm giving myself a break. By hiding in a room alone and writing whispered secrets to you that my daughters will probably discuss with their therapists for years down the road. When they do, here is my on-the-record statement.

Dear girls,

If you didn't act like such assholes to your family, I wouldn't have to write about it.

To keeping it real,
Mom

I kid. Kind of. Maybe not at all, actually.

Other things I've learned to let go of as a mother:

- Picture-perfect wardrobes. I've learned that no matter how much adorableness I put in my girls' closets, they will still pick the Old Navy sequin-flip shirt every damn day. They now both have six items in their summer wardrobes: three Old Navy sequin-flip tees and three pairs of matching shorts. Done.

- The dream that I'll ever be able to be in my bathroom alone again. One hundred percent of the time, my girls come too.

And 50 percent of those times, Nick comes in, trying to cajole them out. This effort has worked 0 percent of the time. Which simply means I end up surrounded by my whole family while trying to literally let my shit go.

- Parent-teacher conferences. I was on a girls' trip during Dorothy's first one and out of town speaking during her second. Which means I inadvertently passed that baton to Nick—and freed myself from the guilt of not going.

- Diets. Yes, in an ideal world, my girls gleefully munch all day on veggies plucked fresh from a garden I tend myself, and they eat organic eggs from chickens we raise. In reality, pizza delivery is in the regular rotation, and we indulge in Happy Meals more often than I'd like to admit. But we're all just making it work, people. Balance, friends. Balance.

- COVID homeschooling fails. I think most moms who parented young children through the pandemic can associate with this: for the first few weeks of quarantine, I taught like a beast. Lots of structure. Virtual guest readers. Baking classes. But I was completely overwhelmed doing it on top of running a business. So I ditched the strict learning schedule, which helped my mental state but left me wondering whether I'm failing my kids. Nick, however, just told me the girls said I was their best teacher ever—a reminder that we are much harder on ourselves than anyone else. Winning.

Speaking of quarantine, this might be my favorite homeschool mom-fail story: so this wonderful momma of three elementary-aged boys was, like many of us, in the thick of quarantine stress when her son told her he couldn't get the camera and microphone working for his class call. As his eight-year-old friends began their conversation, he began to cry. She grew increasingly frustrated. He started yelling at her. She started yelling at the computer.

"What the hell? I am so over this! *What. The. Hell?!*"

The teacher went silent, and twenty sets of eight-year-old eyes went wide.

The camera and mic had worked the entire time.

So she did what she needed to do: she poured herself a glass of wine and let that shit goooooooo.

One pretty day, I took the girls to a playground where dozens of school-age kids were enjoying recess in their pajamas. A third-grade boy—the only kid sporting jeans and a T-shirt—overheard me talking to the girls and confirmed it was pajama day.

"Why aren't you wearing pajamas?" I asked.

"Because my mom doesn't check her emails," he replied.

I laughed—and hoped his mom wasn't sitting in her office beating herself up for missing the pajama-day memo, because her son didn't seem to care a bit.

On another sunny afternoon, I gave myself a time out. It was one I knew I needed, but I waited until the last possible moment to raise my hand and ask for help. I wanted to listen to music and eat a vegetable without anyone touching me. So I went to my favorite café and sat at the bar along the window as Columbus's most fashionable sauntered around the arts district outside. I couldn't help but notice the woman beside me, sitting confidently alone on this weekend afternoon, sipping a Manhattan. I took my headphones off to tell her how much I appreciated her power play. Her next stop, she said, was for a pedi.

She is my prayer for all of us.

Sweet Jesus,

Please help us all to find our sacred Sunday spaces. To give ourselves a break. To let our shit go. And to have friends come to our parties even if a giant tub of cheese balls is the best item on the menu.

Amen.

CHAPTER SIX

Why Me?!
{Get out of Your Own Way}

"Don't take anything personally. Nothing others do is because of you. What others say and do is a projection of their own reality, their own dream. When you are immune to the opinions of others, you won't be the victim of needless suffering."

—Don Miguel Ruiz

I was little—three, maybe four—when my family piled into the station wagon. As my siblings tucked into their spaces, I squeezed between my parents up front.

Thinking I would like the empowerment of pressing the garage door button, Mom asked for a favor.

"Regan," she said, "could you please shut the garage door?"

In a car full of older people, I thought, *How can anyone expect the baby of the fam to get out there, get up there, and get that heavy thing down?*

"Why me?!" I wailed, forlorn.

Everyone burst into laughter. I sobbed.

Sometimes, it feels like people are asking the world when all they want you to do is hit the garage door button. Right?

The truth is the barriers keeping us from goals, dreams, and ultimately joy are often the ones we put in place ourselves. I've unwittingly done it many times throughout my life.

When I finally asked Mark for a divorce, I feared that everyone would abandon me. Not one or two people—all of them. They didn't, of course. Lesson: do not assume the worst.

When I had Dorothy, Nick and I considered moving to the suburbs. Because that's what you do when you have kids. The school question, of course, looms largest. But we love our house. Our neighborhood. Our neighbors. I dig walking to the bakery and the yoga studio and my office. Maybe we don't stay forever. Maybe we do. What I know for sure is that right now, we are happy, and so are those two beautiful kiddos. Lesson: map your own course, and cross each bridge as you get there. You don't have to have tomorrow's answers today.

Once upon a time, with two babies under two and a husband who often travels for work, out-of-town job opportunities felt impossible for me. Nick's family lives in another state, and my mother is in her eighties, not strong enough to care for two babies. I couldn't imagine coordinating care. So I just said no to work travel. Until one day, when a last-minute opportunity to train with internationally celebrated coach Marshall Goldsmith in Salt Lake City presented itself. I moved mountains to secure sitters, threw some clothes in a bag, and jumped on a plane. Everyone survived. And I returned with an entirely new outlook. Lesson: just because it feels impossible doesn't mean it is.

As women, we tend to personalize a lot. A friend doesn't text you back for twenty-four hours? You must have done something awful. Someone whispers to another in a meeting you're leading? They clearly hate your idea. You catch someone yawning during your presentation? You are the world's worst speaker.

But we forget to consider that our friend might be slammed with life and overwhelmed by dozens of text messages she has yet to respond to. Or that the person in the meeting remembered something urgent he needed to communicate and was afraid if he didn't do it now, it would be lost. Or that the person who yawned was up all night with a crying baby and is simply tired.

Also, woe is not you. Nobody likes a martyr. So remove the roadblocks you're putting up yourself, and take control.

My mom wasn't asking me to get my three-year-old body out of the car, find a ladder, climb it, and figure out how to muscle that door to the ground. She was asking me to hit a button.

Stop crying. Get out of your own way and hit it.

OVERCOMING PERFECTION PARALYSIS

Nicole Centeno was pregnant with her first child and laser-focused on being as healthy as she could be. But when she began researching what would be best for her body, she was overcome with anxiety.

Advice was everywhere—and often contradictory.

There's got to be just one thing that I can do right, Centeno thought. *There's got to be just one thing I can do every day that feels good and is genuinely good for me.*

So she started making vegan soups.

Now, her soups (and smoothies) are delivered all over the country.

Instead of being paralyzed by perfection, Centeno took the next best step—and it eventually resulted in her thriving company, Splendid Spoon, a weekly plant-based meal delivery service that ships more than 100,000 meals nationwide every month and grosses $10M a year.

Perfection paralysis: it's the immobilizing fear of failing and something we perfectionists know well. It can wreck our psyche and prevent us from forward movement because we're so scared the results won't *wow* that we're unable to even begin. When it traps us, we end up stressed out—unable to harness our full potential and missing opportunities. It's a lose-lose. Yet still, we end up there.

If the desire to be perfect is holding you back from experiencing something you want in life, consider taking these three simple steps.

Prioritize your energy.

In the throes of perfection paralysis, we often lack perspective.

Take one of my clients, a director of development for a nonprofit. She recently shared that she had an overwhelming list of to-dos both personally and professionally—but was finding it challenging to start on even one. There wasn't enough time to do each perfectly, so she was paralyzed.

She realized as we talked that she was weighing each task equally. Choosing the ideal birthday card for a weekend party seemed just as involved as each task at work, and everything there seemed essential. She also realized she hadn't shared with her boss— whose intelligence is high both intellectually and emotionally— that she was drowning.

Now, she spends time prioritizing her task list. And she meets weekly with her boss so that he can help clear any roadblocks she faces.

Take a global look at your list—and your life. What matters most? Make it perfect. For the rest, let done be good enough.

Let just one thing be good enough.

Problem is, for perfectionists, letting done be good enough is tough. Yes, you understand that perfection is an impossible stan- dard, but that usually doesn't stop you from seeking it. It's a wir- ing thing, right? I'll buy that. But unless you rewire at least a bit, you'll keep banging your head against the same walls. Here's my challenge: today, can you press pause on that unwinnable game and let just one thing be less than perfect?

Maybe it means you send that document up the ladder despite the fact you don't quite love your third page. (Your colleague might have a great idea!) Perhaps it means grabbing fast food for dinner instead of making that pasta you had planned. (Your kids won't die. Promise.) Or it could mean hitting your bed tonight before the house is tidied. (You're probably the only one who will even notice.) Remember our plates-and-napkins conversation? Yes? (Bonus points if you already thought of that.) Good.

What one thing in your life can be good enough today?

Take the next best step.

I have a client taking a bold step to move from survival to purpose mode. She's moving her family across the country to simplify her life. The shift is a year in the making, and it's finally coming to fruition.

She called me in a panic, terrified. She's the family breadwinner, risking their livelihood on a new job and a big dream. She needed to resign. Sell the house. Hire the movers. Research new schools. Choose a new community. Buy a new house. What if it's not all perfect?

I reminded her of her why and encouraged her to take the next best step. So she hired a realtor. And she will keep taking the next best step, one at a time.

In a recent conversation with a TV executive in New York City, I asked about her thoughts on living with perfectionism.

"We as perfectionists impose standards and pressure on ourselves when our audience will never know what did not get done or may not be dialed in enough to appreciate that fine detail we spent hours perfecting," she said. "When we aren't perfect, nobody cares—which is hard to understand because we care so much."

She is also fifty-five and single. She spent her thirties climbing the career ladder and her forties caring for aging parents. There was always going to be thirty pounds to lose and more to get involved in before being perfect for dating.

Finally, she decided to simply take the next best step—and she hired a dating service.

Perhaps this is her vegan soup. Nicole Centeno's next best step turned into a successful business venture. This TV executive's next best step may turn into a meaningful partnership—or even just a few fun dates. My client's next best step is selling her house—and, hopefully, finding the slower pace she seeks. Who knows what yours will bring?

Perfect is impossible. The less we allow ourselves to be paralyzed by impossible expectations, the faster we can move forward—and ultimately reach where we want to go.

Mom

My mom grew up in St. Paul, Minnesota, as America emerged from World War II.

Her dad took rotating shifts in the nightly neighborhood Nazi watch, because apparently, even in suburban Minnesota, fear still lingered. And like most, her family had a victory garden in their yard (where once, while Mom picked veggies, her brother leaned out a window with a BB gun and shot her in the butt).

In her home, there were two priorities: God and education. Mom embraced both. She especially appreciated the opportunities afforded her at her all-girls Catholic school during an era when women didn't usually have equal opportunities.

And she was obsessed with baseball. Her dad, who traveled our hope-filled, postwar America selling books to law firms, often ended up on trains with minor league professional teams. He would score autographed cards of different players to bring home for her.

Occasionally, he would even have players call her on the telephone. Among them was Duke Snider, an eventual all-star who helped lead the Dodgers to six World Series and is now in the National Baseball Hall of Fame.

Mom and her sister had a driver, Reps, who ferried them and other little girls to school since there were gas rations. As they drove, she would daydream about becoming a sportswriter or anchor. But she was born far too soon to pursue such nonsense. Hell, she couldn't even go to law school like her brothers.

So she went to college to be an English teacher. But ho-hum was never her style. (She is, after all, a redhead.) So a few years into school, she applied for a Fulbright scholarship to study overseas.

She was dating a couple of different boys when she dropped her application in the mail.

The first was incredulous.

"You're not going to take it," he said. "Are you?"

The other relished her ambition.

"When you get home," Leo Walsh asked, "will you marry me?"

"Yes," she smiled.

Mom packed her belongings into a trunk, rode a train to New York with friends who were studying in different countries across Europe, and then spent a week on the Atlantic Ocean before arriving in France. She paid someone to carry her trunk up four flights of stairs to her apartment, and she settled in. She studied at the University of Strasbourg by day, wrote letters to Dad by night, and traveled the continent on the weekends, meeting up with friends along the way (all thanks to handwritten notes; their generation was so badass).

When her year was over, she stopped at a fabric shop in New York. She chose a beautiful green material to have a suit made for her going-away wedding outfit. Then, she visited my dad in California, where he was serving in the Air Force. Apparently, absence had only made the heart grow fonder.

Mom and Dad desperately wanted babies. Lots of them. But her body struggled to carry them. She suffered eight miscarriages—including a handful of hemorrhages that threatened her life—over several years.

One of Mom's babies was born at just six months. They named her Mary Dorothy. But in that era, doctors didn't let you hold your baby if they knew it was going to die. So Mom didn't get to touch Mary, let alone snuggle her soft cheeks or kiss her sweet little lips.

"I never got to tell her how beautiful she was," Mom said. "How loved she was."

She's buried beside my grandmother Dorothy in St. Paul.

Mom rarely talks about any of the miscarriages or about Mary. I can't imagine the sorrow in her soul.

Despite it, though, she's always brought the joy, be it with her wicked sense of humor or green pancakes shaped like shamrocks on St. Patrick's Day.

One of my earliest memories is sitting in the living room with her playing Old Maid, just the two of us, with sunlight shining through the window, kissing her strawberry-colored bob, and my blanket on the floor, ready for my nap. And I vividly remember sitting with her at age five, watching Princess Diana marry her prince.

Looking back, I'm amazed at the energy she brought to the table for me—the youngest of the brood. I struggled mightily with spelling. So Mom would make tape recordings of herself saying and then spelling my words, allowing me to listen and learn. It's how I got my spelling down. She has always found a way to meet people where they are.

Mom drinks her coffee a half cup at a time (so it stays piping hot). She cooked dinner from scratch every night. Meatballs and mashed potatoes. Tex-Mex. Tuna melts on Fridays during Lent. She and Dad were especially aggressive corn on the cob lovers; they'd race to see who could finish theirs fastest, and there was never a kernel left.

She taught me the valuable lesson of embracing natural beauty. Once, when we were downtown shopping at Marshall Field's, a woman at the Clinique counter tried talking her into buying a wrinkle cream.

"First, I don't believe it would work," Mom said. "But also, I'm in my fifties. I'm supposed to have wrinkles."

And she never dyed her perfect vibrant red hair—which she's always confidently wore short.

Her one weakness? Her inability to talk vaginas.

I learned about periods, for example, from my sisters, friends, and *Are You There God? It's Me, Margaret*.

Then, our very well-planned sex talk went like this: I was putting the final touches on my makeup for junior prom. My dress was on. My date was in his car, a mile away from pulling in to slip a flower on my wrist and whisk me away.

"Sit down," Mom said. "Your friends are going to pressure you to have sex. Don't do it. They're going to tell you it's good, and it's not."

One minute later, my date picked me up.

(Funny thing is Mom loves sex. She just wasn't raised in a time when you talked about these things. And the idea of her teenage daughter having it out of wedlock? Out of the question.)

And for the trifecta: in high school, I consistently got yeast infections thanks to that silk, bunchy-butt underwear that so many of us wore in the '90s. I didn't know what they were, though, because I couldn't talk to Mom about what was happening. Finally, senior year, I drove to Planned Parenthood—which, as you can imagine, Mom thinks is the devil himself. Thanks to them, though, I learned what my yeast infections were and that ditching that shitty underwear should solve the problem. (It did.)

Thing is had I found myself in a jam—even of the teenage pregnancy variety—Mom would have been a hero. Just like she was when I told her about Amal. Hearing I was dating a woman wasn't the conversation my devout Catholic mom wanted to have. But she turned toward me, not away. Her love is an unconditional, all-encompassing, make-the-effort-to-dye-the-St.-Patty's-Day-pancakes-green-even-for-the-sixth-kid kind of love.

It's how she loved Dad, too—the handsome Air Force officer who encouraged her to spend that year abroad and wrote her sweet letters every week, the husband who shepherded her through all of those emotionally wrecking miscarriages, the father who taught his kids to shoot a basketball and ride bikes. He had a very comfortable job with benefits when he told Mom he wanted to start his own business. She didn't balk; instead, they asked both sets of their parents for loans to help. And then, they built that business together. She never complained about the lean years; I'm not even sure she saw them as that. My parents' company didn't begin making big money until Dad was sixty, and he died at sixty-six.

Dad's death didn't break her, but it tried.

Five years. That's how long after Dad's death she said things were, for her, horrible. She didn't just lose Dad; she lost her community. Most of her social interactions were tied to Dad and the business. People were afraid to reach out, so they didn't.

Then one day, after work, Mom ditched the idea of cooking dinner from scratch and went through the drive-through at Wendy's. She ate her hamburger alone and went to bed without throwing away the wrapper. Nobody but her would know she didn't trash it until morning. Oh, the freedom! Finally, she began to unwind. She started enjoying making choices for nobody but herself—listening to what she wanted, watching whatever she pleased.

Another relationship was out of the question. She wasn't about to become someone's caretaker in her twilight years, nor was she interested in sharing the money she and Dad had worked so hard to earn.

"I'm not going to be a nurse or a purse," she said.

Instead, she is the grandmother who, even in her eighties, gets down on the floor to play with the kids. Who makes holidays super special and ho-hum Wednesday visits extraordinary. She has a collection of teddy bears she got when she was five, and even now, when I take the girls to visit, she hides the bears so the girls can search for them when they arrive. She cruises the TJ Maxx aisles so often to buy little gifts that one day while browsing, when a customer asked an employee where to find something, he said, "I don't know, but go ask that lady. She's here all the time."

My brother Pat, an executive recruiter who regularly visits Columbus for work, often forgoes putting himself and clients up in ritzy hotels and instead takes them to Mom's. She cooks steak for dinner and makes up the guest bed in the basement (where Pat's clients can have a bathroom to themselves). It says an awful lot about her—and, I suppose, Pat—that my brother wants to do business in his parents' home. Especially when it's a modest ranch, and you're hosting Fortune 500 CEOs. But that's the kind of special it is. It's the kind of special she is.

Even as she's aged, her sense of humor has stayed well intact, thank you very much.

When I was still single, my whole family was at the wedding of a dear friend. An adorable young man was flirting with me. In true Walsh form, I started sharing this big story about how my family was super athletic and competed at water volleyball tournaments. (We aren't, and we don't.) My brother Mike walked over.

"I was just telling David about that water volleyball tournament," I said.

"Yeah, funny hobby to some," he ran with it. "But we love it."

Molly eventually popped over and joined the fun.

"And don't let her be modest—she's an absolute star," she said.

Mom sauntered to our table at one point and didn't miss a beat.

"But last tournament," Mom said, "you missed a serve that cost us the game."

It's how we've always rolled. No heads ups. No winking. You just hop aboard the train and ride.

Unsurprisingly, my mom stole the show at my wedding, too, turning her toast into a ten-minute roast. Among other stories, she shared one about the year that every girl, me included, asked Santa for a Cabbage Patch doll. With store shelves empty, she had a friend sew me one.

"It might have been the worst Christmas of our life," Mom deadpanned.

She drew a standing O.

Now, her body is failing her. She is slowly going blind; she had three car accidents in a month and can no longer drive. She's weak on her feet and constantly feels she's going to fall. She can't work, so she's not getting the intellectual stimulation she thrives on. The young adventurer who traveled the world can today barely leave her house. It's incredibly sad.

Yet there she is each night, down on hobbled knees beside her bed, thanking God for all she has.

I love you, Mom.

OWNING YOUR "WHISPER BRAND"

I heard the term for the first time over lunch with an old college advisor. And I love it.

She was telling me about a student in her corporate leadership program. He was smart and capable, but he was unknowingly getting a reputation for his persistent partying. That was his "whisper brand," she said, and it was overshadowing his hard work.

We all have a whisper brand. It's the one articulated by others—good, bad, or otherwise. And since part of getting out of your own way entails knowing exactly who you are and how others perceive you, I want to challenge you to fully understand what your whisper brand is.

Maybe you're the person who is always distracted by your phone when you meet friends for dinner. Or you're the frantic leader who is constantly triple booked, running from one place to the next and making everyone feel short-changed. Or you're the hothead who people fear working with because nobody knows when you'll blow. Or you're perpetually late. Or cheap.

On the flip side, you might be the teammate who always over-delivers. The godmother who remembers birthdays. The CEO who takes five minutes at the start of a meeting to ask about someone's child. The friend who shows up. On time. And grabs the tab.

We are all responsible for how we show up for ourselves and others—all day, every day. We are all responsible for our whisper brand.

So how, exactly, do we own it? Here are three steps to claiming yours.

Step 1: Identify your whisper brand.
Find out what your whisper brand is. How? Have an authentic conversation with a reliable source—a colleague, trusted mentor, or personal friend (*not* someone with an agenda)—who will speak truth to you. Listen before reacting. (Bonus points for asking multiple people to get a clearer and more robust picture.)

Step 2: Live the brand you want to perpetuate.
What DO you want to be known for? Start with your core values. What are yours? And how are your current choices aligned or in conflict with them? What changes can you make to better honor the values you say you hold most dear? Be intentional with where you give your time and with how you nurture your relationships, both professionally and personally.

Step 3: Rinse and repeat.
Hold yourself accountable by sharing your brand goals—and how you plan to better live them out—with someone you trust. Then measure your progress by circling back to the reliable source, or sources, that you talked with in step one. Ask them for feedback on the changes you've made. Check in with yourself, too: How does this version of you feel? How can you continue making minor adjustments that will yield big results?

My college advisor eventually approached her student about his brand of having too much fun to be a serious professional. He accepted her feedback, quieted his partying, stopped showing up tired or hungover, and lived into the brand he wanted to project. He eventually became a productive associate at her company, thanks to successfully changing his whisper brand into one of positivity.

You have a whisper brand, too. What is it? And what do you want it to be?

Lefty

Despite my amazing momma, I grew up feeling less-than because I am a lefty.

I was living in a right-handed world, and everything seemed harder. Using scissors was next to impossible. I have layers of scars to prove how difficult opening cans was. In sports, I'd have to reverse instructions in my head because my stance or lead move would be opposite of what the coach was saying. And don't even get me started on the old-school desks (which, by the way, confronted me again in my thirties when I went to NYU for my coaching program).

I hid behind it and used it as an excuse to the point my mom made it a joke.

"You didn't win the student council election?" she'd say. "Of course not—you're a lefty!"

It gets worse from there. My handwriting was shitty (still is). Between that and my spelling struggles, I gave myself daily belly-aches stressing over whether I'd have to go to the board to write. I knew I would mess up and be humiliated.

I learned differently, too. Never caught on quickly. Sometimes, I wasn't sure if I caught on at all. I went to a reading tutor in third grade because reading was impossibly hard. I spent my entire schooling hoping to go unnoticed. If I was friendly enough and nice enough outside the classroom, maybe nobody would see me hunkered silently into a corner inside of it.

I felt such crippling shame when I scored poorly on standardized tests that it paralyzed me from taking tests because I knew I was bad. I programmed my brain to believe I would never succeed at test-taking; therefore, I didn't. And so the cycle went. When I didn't get into Miami, I felt I had embarrassed not just myself but also my siblings and my parents. I was the only one dumb enough not to make it into the family school.

In other words, I spent the bulk of my childhood filling my brain with head trash. I was different. I was worse.

When applications opened for the annual Miss Arlington contest my junior year of high school, I was intrigued. It was a service-based award with a notable scholarship prize. I had watched other girls do it for years. They applied with essays, and then the finalists stood on stage in beautiful gowns answering questions.

But it's probably just for the pretty girls, I thought. *The popular kids.*

And that wasn't me. I wasn't the prettiest, or the most popular, or certainly the smartest. I was just friends with everybody. But speaking was my jam, and the idea of doing it in front of an audience made my heart do cartwheels.

I tested the idea on my boyfriend.

"I might try out for Miss Arlington," I said, trying to nonchalantly cover my nerves.

"Oh," he said. "You should!"

It's funny, in retrospect, how I was going to let one kind-of-idiotic boy's opinion trump anything I felt in my soul, right? Thank God he pushed me toward a yes.

Because soon, there I was, standing on stage in a prom dress with a white halter top and slimming black skirt, with hundreds of sets of community eyes staring back.

I don't remember a word I said, but I had the crowd in stitches. I winked at my brother Peter as I walked off stage. He was crying he was so proud.

I won the crown—and with it, a college scholarship plus the opportunity to get more meaningfully involved in the community. I volunteered at the community haunted house on Halloween. I painted stars on the blacktop for the Fourth of July. I gave a speech in front of hundreds at the fireworks fest. All because I got out of my own way.

There are enough roadblocks in life. The least we can do is remove the ones we construct ourselves.

Here's to demolition.

CHAPTER SEVEN

Peaches, Please
{Embrace the Now}

"Be happy in the moment, that's enough.
Each moment is all we need, not more."
—Mother Teresa

The family dinner wasn't going as planned.

"I'm trying to let go of being in control," my mother whispered.

"How's that working out for you?" I asked.

"Not very well," she replied.

My mom fully owns her need to control situations—specifically family dinners. Where people sit, what they eat, how much time we need to sit and visit before a meal is served, and just how they generally go down. I've witnessed this for over forty years—not in a bad way, just aware that my mom likes things to play out a certain way (hers).

I can't really blame her for this desire to control. She's good at being in charge. She successfully raised six kids, ran a business with Dad, and when Dad died, she ran the family and the business.

The challenge is control freaks can get so caught up in their vision that they miss the moment they've planned so hard to create.

At dinner, for example, my mom was upset that half the family was eating while standing in the kitchen, not while sitting in the dining room, where she wanted them. But they were having a ball—talking, laughing, watching the kids. And isn't that the point of family dinners? So what if it wasn't happening the way she orchestrated? The joy and togetherness she ultimately wanted to feel was indeed happening. She just needed to step back so she could see it.

Recently, as Mom and I talked about some of her upcoming medical appointments and procedures, she lamented a brutal observation.

"Most of life," she said, "is waiting for events to pass."

I felt sad because she's my mom, and I don't like seeing her in physical or emotional pain. But my sadness is also rooted in guilt because despite coaching others out of this trap, I, too, have found myself occasionally wishing time would just speed up. (I see you, toddler parents. And I have a pretty baller liquor cabinet should you need to visit.) My husband recently acknowledged that he often feels this way, too. He worries constantly about clients, expectations, and performance, always just trying to make it to the next week.

Many of us do it. I know, because I spend my days with women feverishly running on their hamster wheels, working so hard to get to next that they completely miss now, asking if this is it.

Truth is we all control the pace of our own lives. There is not actually "so little time." Everyone gets the same twenty-four hours a day. And each of us chooses how we use it and controls how and when we stop to savor the now.

Sometimes, for me, that means putting my phone in another room and taking my daughter on the porch in the afternoon sun, singing songs and playing together, just the two of us. Other times, it means asking Nick to feed the girls so I can walk to my favorite restaurant and eat solo at the bar. Many nights, it means closing our laptops, putting the girls to bed early, opening a good bottle of wine because it's Tuesday, and retreating to the porch for a date.

Of course, embracing the now means leaning into moments that are uncomfortable, too. Like the stretch of time when doctors were trying to fix my pee problem, and I had to do private part exercises while counting Mississippis. Or the first time I went into labor, which included a locked hospital entrance, a tow-away zone, a metal detector (Nick set it off three times), and an elevator incident with a woman wearing an orange jumpsuit and shackles. (Exactly as we had planned!)

But this is life, friends. And the good news is if we can get good at embracing the uncomfortable moments, we can really relish the ones that make the highlight reel.

At my very first job, while working with Colleen on event production, I was the youngest staffer on the team—and the first to close a deal on a new initiative. The CEO gave me a $1,000 bonus.

"Don't just blow it on clothes," she advised. "Make an experience."

There were all sorts of reasons to simply shop. But my parents were heading to southern France, so I found a plane ticket for $500 and crashed with them at their rental home in a town called La Garde-Freinet. We shopped together in markets. We went to a beach in St. Tropez carrying a table umbrella we had mistaken for a beach umbrella—plus an ax to properly lodge it in the sand. We picnicked on our blanket, overlooking yachts bobbing gently on the stunning water, eating fresh peaches and olive tapenade.

I couldn't have known that in a couple of short months, Dad would be dead.

But I had embraced the now, choosing an adventure over shoes, and what a choice it was.

A MILLION LITTLE THINGS

There was a new network show premiering with a preview that played continuously before it launched.

"They say friendship isn't one big thing," it said. "It's a million little things."

That's the name of the show: *A Million Little Things*. The premise is this: There is a group of tight-knit adult friends. One kills himself. The others are upset they didn't see it coming. The show explores friendship, love, and humanness—in other words, a lot of the stuff we forget to nurture between rushing to work and shuffling the kids to bed so we can hop back on our laptops and finish those presentations...only to start over again in the morning.

Meanwhile, in the days leading up to the show's premiere, I couldn't help but make a connection to the emails flowing into my inbox:

- *"I'm so sorry I had a meeting that went over and wasn't able to make this today—so much to do so little time!"*

- *"My schedule has been so busy...last minute things keep coming up that need immediate attention."*

- *"I feel like I'm a butler to my children...I have no time for myself."*

And there it is—the trap. We're in constant motion, but nothing seems to change: we're overprogrammed and underwhelmed.

This message is another reminder that you control the pace of your life. If you've written an email like one of my favorites above, or if you feel like you could, consider this:

- There is not actually "so little time." Everyone gets the same twenty-four hours a day. And each of us chooses how we use it.

- If your schedule is busy, it's because you've created that. So either embrace it or change it. But don't use it as an excuse. (Also, if last-minute things keep coming up that require immediate attention, perhaps you could be more proactive about planning and prioritizing.)

- Feel like a butler to your children? You are the parent, which means you are in charge. Create an environment where you thrive, because that will, in turn, allow you to be a parent that helps them thrive. After all, if you teach a man to fish...yeah, you get it.

Friends, take a breath. Remember that controlling the pace of your life (and ultimately your happiness) all comes back to understanding what it is you want and why you want it. Next step? Say no without guilt to things that won't get you there. (For me, that's happy hours, charity functions, and kids' birthday parties, to name a few.) And say yes with purpose to things that will. (I consistently give noes to those happy hour and charity opportunities to savor quality family time—so when a company like QuickBooks called and asked me to fly out to California for an engagement, it was an easy yes without feeling like I was short-changing my husband or kids.)

The TV show's line is right. Friendship is not just one big thing—it is a million little things. And so is life.

I want to enjoy all those million little things that make it worth living. I want to wake up every morning, kiss my babies, and have a workout and coffee before ever checking my phone. I want to have a minute for a client's call to celebrate her major work win. I want to savor wine with my husband on the front porch after we put the girls to bed. And I want the same for you.

What are you not noticing right now or enjoying right now because you're so caught in the busy grind that you're never fully present? Friendship is a million little things. Life is a million little things.

Control your pace so that you can notice them. And relish them.

Kelly

I had been on a date or two with the firefighter when he called out of the blue.

"Want to have dinner tonight at the fire station?" he asked.

"Sure," I said. "Can I bring a friend?"

I knew before I hung up that Kelly would say yes, despite the fact it was her wedding week. Because Kelly is the friend who is always in. The friend you want in a good time. The friend you want in a bad time. The friend you want when you need something creative, or something fixed, or something hard. I mean, she's never going to show up on time, which may be because she sucks so much marrow out of every second that transitioning to the next thing is apparently incredibly challenging. (Also, seriously, Kelly: answer a fucking text.) But nobody eats and breathes and laughs and lives in the moment like Kelly does.

Kelly and I met in third grade and eventually formed the Garfield Club with a few other neighborhood kids. We met in Kelly's playhouse, where I was in charge of taking notes, and sold Kool-Aid and Rice Krispies Treats on the corner. After college, she accepted a magazine gig in New York, making less than $20,000 a year, a gamble she hoped would pay off. Thanks to her almost-nonexistent salary, she lived in Jersey City—even further from the city than me.

As we navigated the start of adulthood and our dreams, we treated ourselves to Magnolia Cupcakes and met at White Horse Tavern for beers. Once, I told her I was flying home to visit my family.

"I'll take you to the airport," she offered.

The time was inconvenient, the traffic is always a nightmare, and just generally speaking, nobody in New York offers to take anybody to the airport—especially via Hoboken. Except for Kelly. She's just that kind of good human. The same kind who, after you've both moved back to Columbus, says, "I'll be ready in ten" when a good-looking firefighter invites you to a last-minute dinner.

We listened intently as the guys walked us on a tour through the station. We giggled as we crawled into uniforms ourselves—pants, jacket, boots, hat. Kelly smashed her pile of thick red hair beneath a helmet, turned to me, and roared. We helped make pizzas and laughed our way through dinner. The guys must have hated the diamond on her finger. But for that moment, at least, she was theirs, and she was mine, and how lucky all of us were.

Kelly's magazine gamble had paid off, and she was rewarded with a high-paying, literally high-flying position as Creative Director at a posh national firm based in our hometown. She helped me land a job there, too.

We ended up testing for our Muay Thai shorts on the same night. When I drove her home, I told her I was going to tell Mark I wanted a divorce. She not only helped me navigate my dissolution, but she also wrote a note to the Catholic Church on my behalf as part of the process. She introduced me to Vieques. She fully supported my dating Amal. (When I told my mom about Amal, she said, "You have too much pizzazz to be a lesbian." Kelly immediately bought me a t-shirt that said *pizzazz*). When I bought my condo, she painted swatches of paint all over my house to help choose my vibe. (And then, when I chose it, she decorated the whole damn place.)

After Nick proposed, Kelly came to the wedding seamstress with me to learn how to bustle my gown, and she was the only person I allowed to help me get ready on the big day. She nestled my fascinator on my head, perfected my veil, zipped my dress.

I found out I was pregnant on May 4, and at a Cinco de Mayo party the next day, Kelly—who by then had a one-year-old son and was pregnant with her second—became the first person aside from Nick I told. She promptly created and sent a PDF of everything I would and wouldn't need for Baby Number One. And knowing that I was nauseous and unable to eat much other than candy, she dropped off a five-pound bag of gummy bears before I headed to New York for my coaching courses that summer.

Kelly is a workaholic by nature, and she's brilliant at what she does. But she's equally passionate about being a wife and parent, both of which she does the same way she does everything else— big and all in. Impromptu dinners in Chicago. Weekend shows in New York. Family adventures to hike and fish in Canada. Matching, elaborately themed Halloween costumes. Human-sized Hungry Hungry Hippos games. Semi-dangerous wintertime sledding. They are whacky, unpredictable, and the life of the party (which they're usually hosting). The first time she tried taking a weeklong trip away from her oldest, she ended up leaving halfway through. That's the kind of fervor with which she loves her boys.

One night, Kelly and I dined with a friend, toasting the new, big job she had just begun with a billion-dollar tech darling. She mentioned that her youngest son—then three years old—had been randomly throwing up in the middle of the night. The pediatrician couldn't pinpoint a problem. But if it happens again, he advised, take him to the emergency room.

A few hours after we finished our dinners, her son began vomiting again. Kelly's husband took him to the ER while she stayed home with their firstborn. He called in the middle of the night, panicked.

"Get here immediately," he said.

A doctor pulled them into a room alone, Kelly still in her pajamas, shaken.

"Your son," he said, "has a brain tumor."

There was a blur of scans and doctors and research, and suddenly, in thirty-six hours or forty-eight hours—what are hours anymore?—her baby was in the operating room, his head cut open, with doctors carefully removing the demon inside.

Kelly soon found herself in the ICU, beside a bed that cradled her unconscious son, listening to the soundtrack of beeping monitors. Worrying. Praying. Pleading. It was another day before she could even pull herself away from his bed to the family waiting room. She dragged her feet there in the middle of the night and started reviewing emails that were slowly piling up in her inbox. It was, as usual, filled with a series of requests for favors. Among her nonwork-related requests in just two days alone:

- Design a logo
- Have her baby crib
- Hook someone up with a job
- Send email addresses for a party invite
- Design a patch for a summer camp
- Discuss a job description
- Recommend candidates for an open position at a major retailer
- Meet up for a lunch to network
- Donate to a school silent auction
- Officiate a wedding

Any other week, it would have been perfectly normal for her to get to all of those requests. But there, under the florescent hospital lights on an uncomfortable chair, wearing the same pajamas she had worn for days, Kelly's utter exhaustion brought clarity.

Fuck, she thought. *I give way more than I receive.*

Suddenly, the woman who always says yes realized that she was sprinting a marathon of her own design and that she needed to shut it down. Or at least back off the pace she had set. Some of those people, she realized, would have been totally fine with "No." They wouldn't take it personally. Why was she?

Of course, few people knew she was even in the hospital. As they found out, the requests fizzled for a few weeks. But they slowly began ramping up again.

So Kelly outlined what areas and relationships she would give extra time and energy to and what areas and relationships she wouldn't. To this day, there are people she cut off because of that night in the hospital—not as friends, but as recipients of "extra." She also time-boxes her extras, so every extra has a limit.

Every few months, Kelly reevaluates who and what gets her extra. And it shifts—different people, different forms of self-care, different relationships with colleagues, new ways of interacting with her kids as they grow and change.

You're never going to change the wiring of a woman who sky-dives on her fortieth birthday or buys matching neon ski suits for friend getaways to Jackson Hole. I mean, she is a redhead, with a level of spice I know all too well (insert Mom dumping the boy-friend who resented her mission to study abroad here). But despite the fact her son has fully recovered, Kelly still carries that list of ICU favor requests with her as a daily reminder that she only has so much time to spend, and she needs to choose wisely how she spends it.

Spreading it so widely had a smaller impact on individuals and exhausted her, she realized. Now, she's still exhausted, she jokes. But she's at least more confident her efforts are paying off.

That means that the human who is better than anyone I know at relishing every moment is now relishing only the most meaningful.

What a gift that I still get to live in some of those moments with her.

WHEN EVERYTHING FEELS URGENT, CHOOSE SIGNIFICANT INSTEAD

Quarantine.

Years from now, that word will inevitably trigger a flood of memories and emotions for all of us. But as I type, we're still in the thick of it. Hell, we may still be by the time this book goes to press. So I'm sharing my thoughts, as I think the lessons we learn in navigating this will help us in all sorts of circumstances down the road.

Anyway, despite all the ways that our lives have dramatically slowed during this time (or, in some cases, come to a complete standstill), I think it's safe to say most of us feel a sense of urgency.

We urgently want to make sure our kids are experiencing some semblance of a routine. We urgently want to find ways to be productive and use this time wisely. And we urgently want things to return to "normal."

I feel it, too—the desire to press fast-forward on what is clearly a very uncomfortable moment for all of us. And if we're honest, we do this a lot in life, don't we? We buy into the concept of living in the moment when the moment feels good (I'm looking at you, birthday celebrations and beach vacations). But when the moment gets uncomfortable (illness, death, job loss), we're not so into the concept then. But right now—or whenever we're in trying times, whatever those may be—I think putting down our heads and charging forward is a mistake.

Stop living urgent and start living significant.

Susan Adams wrote that in a Forbes blog about productivity that I read a while back, and it stopped me in my tracks. I jotted it down. Now, it feels more applicable than ever.

Because now is not the time to rush around, cluttering our days with shoulds and screens and avoiding how we really feel about the losses we've experienced, the incredible challenges ahead, and the tension between what we want to be and what is.

We need to let go of that urgent way of living and let those feelings come, honoring our truth so that we can step into more significant living.

In Glennon Doyle's book *Untamed*, I think her description of significant living is spot-on: the truest, most beautiful lives we can imagine.

It's a grounded way of being. Not necessarily an easy way of being, but a much more meaningful way of being. Being present isn't a struggle. Knowing and honoring our priorities takes precedent. And the people who matter most know it.

Moving from urgent to significant isn't a simple task, however, especially when our society is so clearly in crisis.

But it starts with acknowledging our discontent, as Glennon writes:

> *Discontent is evidence that your imagination has not given up on you. It is still pressing, swelling, trying to get your attention by whispering: "Not this."*

We're all experiencing a heavy dose of "Not this," and now is the time to tune in. Start writing down what feels uncomfortable and what a better present and future might look like. Talk it out with a partner or friend. Put your imagination in conversation with your discontent.

I've also noticed a heavy dose of self-imposed guilt making the rounds lately. We feel bad for feeling angry, sad, or anxious about our current circumstances because others have it worse. (And then we urgently try to avoid that guilt by completing tasks or mindlessly scrolling social media.)

But as my friend Alexis Joseph so wisely put in her recent post, pain is not a competition.

Pain is relative, and you're allowed to feel it. In fact, I encourage you to. Just don't let it run the show.

Here's to ditching the urgent, and choosing the significant.

Peeing My Pants

One Halloween night in Hoboken, my friends Betsey, Jamie, and I dressed as flappers and crashed a party. We laughed about it so hard on our way home that I wet myself. But Betsey did, too, so it didn't seem like a problem so much as a one-time thing clearly spurred by our hilarity.

When I started Muay Thai, though, I noticed that I tinkled a little bit every time I did high knees. Every time I kicked a bag. Every time I took a punch to the stomach. I started wearing a pad—the thick kind, like our moms wore—with double underwear and my shorts, desperately hoping to contain the urine. I mean, thankfully, most people sweat puddles and smell terrible, but I was mortified.

Later, when I joined a different gym, burpees became my nemesis. Up for a jump, down for a push-up, up for a jump, down for a push-up. My squirts of pee would begin pooling on the mat almost immediately. I padded up, wore only black pants, and prayed.

It happened so often my stories are nearly limitless. The night my friend Nikki and I ate at the Rossi and went to a drag show at Axis, I laughed so hard that I peed my pants on High Street. After one particularly fun dinner with our friends Michael and Doug, I emptied my bladder in hysterics as we walked, and I literally squeaked the whole way home. Ruined my sandals.

It took years to ask my doctor for help. I mean, what woman who hasn't even birthed a child tinkles with every sneeze?

The diagnostic exam was almost as embarrassing as the problem itself. Doctors hooked something onto my urethra and sat me on a chair with a hole in it. They filled my bladder with a liquid and then asked me to cough, to sneeze, and eventually to stand and jump— naked—looking for leaking as I did. I was horrified.

Physical therapy for my bladder—which, no surprise, was thin and weak—wasn't much better. I worked with a woman who inserted what were essentially dildos into my vagina and had me squeeze them with my bladder muscles for a certain number of Mississippis.

One Mississippi, two Mississippi, three Mississippi, release. One Mississippi, two Mississippi, three Mississippi, release.

She instructed me through Kegels, too, and gave me exercises to try at home.

Nothing worked.

Finally, they gave me what is basically Botox in my bladder. And oh, sweet relief.

Of course, just like Botox in your forehead, Botox in your lady parts wears off over time. So post-kiddos, I went in for another surgery. They sent me home with a catheter and bladder bag.

When it wouldn't drain, I ended up making a late-night emergency call to a doctor friend, so before I knew it, dearest Doug was up in my vag trying to get the catheter to drain. I mean, if that's not the sign of a true friend, I'm not sure what is.

The next day, as I ventured to the hospital to have the catheter removed, I disguised my tube of flowing urine with a maxi dress and tucked the yellow-filled bladder bag inside a grocery bag. (To connect the dots with an earlier story: sitting in my car that day is when *Harvard Business Review* called with the news I was being published. Cheers!)

I noted my long dress and grocery bag, telling the doctor how embarrassed I was.

"I have power executives in here all the time for this problem, and they hide it amazingly," he said. "You wouldn't believe how I've seen people conceal this."

Guess what? More than one in four women over eighteen suffers from incontinence. Which means a whole bunch of us are dealing with this and not saying a word.

Moral: if too many of your moments are punctuated by pee, call your doctor. Your favorite sandals are begging you to. Your workout partners may be, too.

LETTING GO OF CONTROL

But they are supposed to be sitting at the dining room table. On chairs. Using inside voices.

That's what my mom was thinking as she stood beside me at the family party, watching my siblings gobble food over the kitchen island and roar with laughter as she grew more irritated by the minute.

It's easy to judge when we see the picture painted from the outside, isn't it? Come on, lady. They're all having fun. Let it go!

Yet most of us have areas of our lives we long to control too, don't we? Problem is we lack perspective. As a result, we often fail to recognize how our controlling desires impact our mood, our productivity, and our relationships.

The next time you want to control a situation, pause and ask yourself these two questions:

1. **How do I want to feel right now?** Sometimes elevating out of the moment and seeing the bigger picture can help you loosen your grip. At dinner, for example, my mom was

upset that half the family was eating while standing in the kitchen—not while sitting in the dining room, where she wanted them. But they were having a ball—talking, laughing, watching the kiddos. And isn't the point of family dinners exactly that? So what if it wasn't happening the way she orchestrated? It was still happening. The joy and togetherness she ultimately wanted to feel was indeed happening. She just needed to step back so she could see it. If things aren't panning out how you want, determine what you can do to change that.

2. **What is my best and highest use right now?** You only have so much energy. Control freaks can easily misspend theirs by obsessing over things that others can handle—or may even handle better. If you must control something, choose that something wisely. Delegate or let go of the rest—or pay the price. A former colleague of mine, for example, liked to control every single detail of projects, and it was detrimental to the team. Projects that should have taken days turned into months, with endless rounds of revisions. It slowed the organization down and caused tension with vendors and business partners. Identify your best and highest use and spend your energy there.

You can't control it all. Asking these two simple questions, however, can offer the perspective we sometimes need.

And no matter what, remind yourself that the one thing you can control is your reaction to any situation.

Sit back—or, rather, stand up—and raise your glass.

It's a...Lesson

You know how people have a birth plan? Like a whole thing they write out about how it's all going to go down? They list the specific scents they want wafting through the delivery room, and the music they want softly playing, and yada yada yada. Yeah. I never had one of those. I didn't even do a single birthing class. Or read a book. I had Kelly's PDF, after all. What more could I need?

So at thirty-nine weeks pregnant, I visited my doctor for my regular checkup.

"You're still not close," she said. "See you next week."

I went to my barre studio and crushed a class. I wondered what my little boy would look like. What he would act like. I tried not to hate the ultrasound tech who had accidentally ruined the gender surprise months ago when she called the baby a "he." I never told Nick.

That night, Nick and I walked to Chipotle for dinner. I ordered spicy salsa on my burrito bowl. It was delish.

Back home, Nick settled in on the couch with a glass of bourbon and a show I wasn't interested in, so I went to our room.

Damn, I thought when the first cramp came. *I shouldn't have had the spicy salsa.*

Soon, I was on my hands and knees, irritated at myself. Why the spicy salsa at thirty-nine weeks? Moron. I mean, I obviously wasn't in labor. My doctor just said so.

An hour later, Nick walked upstairs.

"This is weird, but I'm having really big pains," I said. "And they're six minutes apart."

I finally called the doctor.

"You're definitely in labor," she said. "When the contractions get closer together, come in."

I realized, horrified, that I wasn't sure I had a single photo of me pregnant. What kind of mother am I? I'm fucking failing, and I haven't even begun!

"Get your phone and take my picture," I told Nick. I breathed my way through standing up, slowly pulling off my shirt, and turning to the side. (Yes—that snapshot of me wearing a nursing bra and underwear remains the defining photo documentation of Dorothy's time in my belly.)

Suddenly, my entire body started convulsing. I threw on pants, and we made our way to Nick's car. We both thought they told us on the hospital tour that if you went into labor after hours, you should go to the emergency room. We obviously hadn't been listening closely. So we went to the ER, where Nick parked in a tow-away zone to escort me in, my body still shaking uncontrollably. I could barely walk through the metal detector. Neither could Nick; he set it off not one time, not two times, but three times—keys, change, belt buckle. Then security told him he had to move his car.

I stood in the mile-long line with the shakes.

"Can we let her go ahead of us?" someone finally yelled. (Bless you, angel soul, wherever you are.)

Soon, a nurse was pushing me through the hallways in a wheelchair. Nick was still in the parking lot, regretting his poor listening skills. WTF.

"Good luck!" someone hollered, still coming down from an obvious drug high.

We waited for an elevator to open. When it did, a woman in an orange jumpsuit and shackles who had burnt someone's house down and suffered wounds in the process was walking off. Of course!

My stomach churned the entire ride up. The maternity floor desk clerk started asking questions.

"And what's your husband's—"

"I'm going to get sick," I cut her off, then proceeded to barf up every ounce of my Chipotle between the remainder of her check-in questions.

With only one anesthesiologist in the building, the epidural I so desperately wanted was still two hours from happening. Thankfully, Nick finally showed.

"Please help me," I pleaded. There was nothing he could do.

Thank God they didn't check my measurements until after the epidural, because once they did, they said I was ready to rock. My doctor was off-duty. So a woman I'd never met walked in and promptly got up in my vagina. As did an ER doctor who wanted to see the birth. And a small handful of medical students. Why, again, did we pick a teaching hospital?

I wondered whether I would be doing this for the next seven hours. Or fifteen. Or twenty-four.

Nick stood at my shoulder and counted, a job he took incredibly seriously.

"One...two...three...puuuuusssssshhhh," he coached.

Three good pushes were all it took.

"It's a girl!" the doctor said.

It's a…what? It took me a second to recalibrate.

They swaddled my tiny babe and rested her on my chest.

I got my surprise after all.

It didn't go down as I had envisioned, despite the fact my expectations were never very high. And it was punctuated with the sadness that Dad wouldn't be there to meet his sweet granddaughter. (This is the crippling truth about loss: you experience it over and over.) But just as I had savored the sweet simplicity of those peaches beneath an awkward umbrella held in place by an ax on the beach with Mom and Dad in St. Tropez, I fully lived into the uncomfortable hilarity and warm surprise of Dorothy's arrival.

Because if we only embrace the perfect, we miss most of the fun.

Who cares if nobody's eating in the dining room, right?

Get off the hamster wheel, Mom, and enjoy the party.

CHAPTER EIGHT

F*@$ the Rules

{Always Take the Next Best Step}

"Do what makes you feel good, because there'll always be someone who thinks you should do it differently. Whether your choices are hits or misses, at least they're your own."
—Michelle Obama

I had paralysis by analysis.

I knew I wanted to coach others. But I wasn't yet forty, and another coach told me that until I was, I wouldn't have credibility. I was also trying to get pregnant with my first baby, which isn't exactly an advisable time to launch a business.

Then, the insane-but-doable meeting happened. If camp wanted to execute back-to-back fundraisers with an already-depleted staff, awesome. But I would not be doing it with them.

So I finally did precisely what I would have coached anyone else to do. I took the next best step.

I scheduled an appointment with my therapist, talked it out, and mapped a plan. I danced my way out of bed within two days. I enrolled in New York University's prestigious coaching program within two weeks. And I hugged my camp friends goodbye long before those back-to-back fundraisers.

I can't start coaching yet; I'm too young. I can't sacrifice six weeks of paid maternity leave; that's stupid. I can't...I can't...I can't.

It was similar to the story I had told myself years ago.

I can't leave this job. It's secure. The benefits are great. And my stock options might double someday. Or triple. Could they quadruple?

I repeated those words to myself for five years in a corporate job. Five. I hated that job. But for all of the reasons listed above, I felt I had to stay, despite my unhappiness. I didn't have a choice. Sound familiar?

It's so easy to convince ourselves that we don't have a choice, isn't it? If I've learned anything from my own lived experiences and those I coach, it's that we're very good at tuning into societal norms, the opinions of others, and fear of the unknown when we make our decisions. We let them tell us what we should do, and you know how I feel about shoulds.

This does two very bad things: It makes us feel trapped in jobs, relationships, and situations that aren't suited for us. And it removes our autonomy, stripping our ability to make decisions using our gut as our guide. After all, our gut often asks us to do scary things—things that make us uncomfortable—and it's easier to tell ourselves "I have no choice."

But we're always choosing, even when we think we aren't.

Every time we wake up and go to a job we hate, we're choosing. Every time we avoid hard conversations with loved ones, we're choosing. Every time we ignore our intuition and say yes to shoulds, we're choosing.

Find what you want. And take the next best step to getting there.

YOU: THE REBOOT

A friend of mine recently forwarded me an article from *The Onion* that I can't stop laughing about: "Man Returns to Work after Vacation with Fresh, Reenergized Hatred for Job."

"I'm rested, my batteries are recharged, and I'm ready to despise my entire professional life more intensely than ever before!" the story says.

I have a vivid memory of taking two weeks off from the camp job that was no longer a good fit for me. The day I went back to work, I looked outside at the snow-covered roads and started crying.

"This," my husband said, "is the last winter you will ever do this job."

In that moment, it clicked—I was 100 percent responsible for my happiness and success. I needed to let go of the job that no longer brought me joy. I needed to find my next.

Finding your next can be scary. You know what's scarier? Living a life despising the majority of your day.

If going to work brings literal tears, here are three ideas for forging ahead.

Make professional dating your side hustle.

Feeling stuck and don't know what your next move should be? Connect with as many people as you can outside of your current network. Who do you admire? Who is doing interesting work? Who is passionate about their career? Feed off the energy of people who are inspired by their work, and use it to propel you toward your next.

Think impact over income.

One of the most transformative chapters of my professional career—taking that camp job—initially required me to take a 40 percent decrease in my salary. I almost didn't take it because I was afraid to lose the income. So many of us put blinders on to incredible opportunities because they may require taking a step backward in pay or title. I offer this perspective: put a value on what you'll gain by being energized by your work. Does that value make up for the difference in income or title? My experience: within a year, I was able to earn the 40 percent back by proving my worth to the organization (and making a case for a raise I deserved). I also was able to make an incredible impact through my work, which brought an enormous amount of satisfaction and pride in how I spent my time. Win-win.

Set boundaries.

I understand that finding your next can take some time, so one way to protect your energy is to set better boundaries with your employer. Reset expectations about your availability by cutting back on after-hours communication. Turn off email notifications on your phone. Consider giving yourself a one-week trial of not checking email in the morning before going to your office. Use this found time instead to sit down and enjoy breakfast without a screen in front of you. If you start your day from a place of positivity, it can dramatically improve how the day plays out.

No matter how stuck you feel, you aren't. Rebooting can be intimidating. But it can also change everything—literally. And the only one who can hit the button is you.

♥

Cynthia Stamps

Life was heavy.

I had quit the big firm and was still unemployed, aside from the part-time job at our family business. Amal and I were mostly off, but not off completely, which was confusing. I felt lost and overwhelmed.

I visited my therapist, who encouraged me to balance out my aggressive Muay Thai practice and boot camps with something softer. "You need to breathe," she said. She recommended I visit Reiki Specialist Cynthia Stamps.

Reiki is a Japanese healing technique meant to reduce stress and prompt relaxation. It's grounded in the idea that practitioners can channel energy into patients by soft and strategic touches on or around your body. It's less massage and more laying of the hands, if you will.

Seemed a bit sketchy to me—I mean, is it just a lazy massage?—but I figured it was worth a try.

I walked up the drive of Cynthia's charming cottage. She had converted her garage into a soundproof studio where she and her husband trained their troupe of flamenco dancers. Special guitars that her husband had handcrafted rested gently on stands in the corner. In the center of the room, she had set up a massage table, where she would perform Reiki on me.

Cynthia was petite, with a mound of black curly hair, wise eyes, and a radiant smile. She carried the confidence of a woman in her fifties, like she knew all the secrets, like you wanted to tell her yours.

"I've been through the wringer," I said. "I got married when I shouldn't have, and I got divorced..."

Embarrassment dripped down my cheeks.

"Congratulations," Cynthia said firmly. "Good for you!"

She was thrilled I'd left a marriage that wasn't right for me, she said. That took guts.

I told her about everything—Amal, work, confusion. I told her I felt embarrassed, afraid. She smiled. "You've made so many difficult choices," she said. "But you're being true to you. That," she said, "is amazing." Cynthia made me feel like a warrior.

I wiped my tears, lay on the table, closed my eyes, and exhaled. Sometimes, I could feel her hands land gently on my arms or my head. Other times, I could feel them hovering above my chest or stomach. I drifted in and out of consciousness. Then, it felt like I was levitating, floating on clouds.

The power of her energy healing is indescribable. It was juicy, exotic. It made me feel at ease, hopeful, happy. Despite my limited budget, I began going as often as I could afford it—sometimes once a month, other times once a week. Once, I remember feeling like other people were in the room, like there was a host of hands on me. Were they angels? Spirits? I didn't know. Didn't care. Just felt loved, safe.

Being with Cynthia was like being wrapped in a hug of sunshine. She had a way about her that was special, magical.

She taught me Reiki's Five Precepts:

- *Just for today I release all anger.*
- *Just for today I release all worry.*
- *Today I am grateful.*
- *Today I live each moment in the present and do my work honestly.*
- *Today I show kindness to all that has life.*

That mantra became a crucial part of my morning routine.

It didn't just get me through a trying stretch. It changed the way I think. Today is all we have, anyhow. We mustn't be dreaming so far forward that we miss it.

My all-time favorite gift is a poem Cynthia shared with me by His Holiness the XIV Dalai Lama. It speaks of the wild divinity in us all, of the angel of memory, of trusting the wisdom within our souls.

Along with the poem, she gifted me a ninety-minute recording of the Dalai Lama chanting. I would listen to it in my condo all alone—this beautiful music transforming me.

Two years after we met, Cynthia was diagnosed with breast cancer. She died at sixty.

Her funeral was held at a park. It was an amazing celebration of an extraordinary woman—flamenco dancing, singing, joy. I sat beside my therapist for the service, filled with gratitude to have known and experienced a true healer at the moment I needed healing.

Cynthia is with me still, every day. I've adapted her "just for today" mantra to fit my daily challenges or opportunities, and I suggest my clients do the same. Facing a big presentation? Say to yourself, "Just for today, I am confident." Overwhelmed with what-ifs about the future? Say, "Just for today, I will savor right now." Feeling trapped in a relationship? Escape for a long walk alone and say, "Just for tonight, I am free."

We are not victims relegated to shame or embarrassment at wherever we are. We are warriors.

And we can do anything just for today.

Brave before Good

She stood on the edge of the high dive in her polka-dotted swimsuit, her seven-year-old legs trembling.

"It's so scary!" she screamed through her tears.

She had stood in line for over an hour, urging other kids to go ahead of her for two straight swim periods.

"You don't have to jump," said her mom, who stood behind her.

"But I really want to!" she cried.

I was in the diving bay, waiting to catch my daughter, who was next in line.

"What's your name?" I called up to the girl.

"Harper," she said.

"Well, Harper, my name is Regan," I said. "And I believe in you. I know this is scary. But I can catch you if you'd like. You can do this."

"I'm so scared," she cried.

"I get it. I get scared too," I said. "But you don't have to do this alone. When you're ready, I'm going to be right here. I'm going to count to three, and then you're going to jump, okay?"

She nodded hesitantly.

"One...two...three!"

She paused.

And then she jumped.

Applause erupted. "Way to go, Harper!" someone cheered.

It was glorious.

You've got to be brave before you can be good.

I heard the line in a movie once and liked it so much I made Nick pause the film so I could write it down.

Brave before good: that's what sweet Harper had to be that day on the diving board. And that's what we all have to be so often in life.

It's a better way, in my estimation, to say *Fake it 'til you make it.* Because if you're doing something—anything, really—you're inherently, then, not faking it. You're doing it. You may not be doing it well. Probably because it's new to you. But *Fake it 'til you make it* implies you're somehow hoodwinking people, yourself included. I'd like to challenge that notion. Because I think if you're trying something you're not good at, you're not faking anything: you're simply dialing up your guts and being brave.

I've done it so many times. Moving to New York. Learning to live without Dad. Leaving my first marriage. Getting in the Muay Thai ring. Opening a camp with a bunch of people who had never opened a camp. Becoming a wife (again). Having babies. Launching a business.

In every one of those instances, I felt like Harper, standing on the edge of a board, shaking and terrified. But each time I jumped, someone caught me. Someone clapped for me. And someone else— usually a whole lot of someones, actually—cheered me on.

Sure, Becky from your high school is a royal asshole on Facebook who knows exactly how everyone should be parenting, working, voting, and living. But Becky aside, the world is filled with people, and especially women, who are pretty wonderful. They're not just rooting for you to jump—they're ready to celebrate when you do.

WHEN IN DOUBT, LOOK TO YOUR STRENGTHS

In a world that glorifies a busy schedule and encourages us to keep moving that measuring stick a little farther forward, it's easy to lose our sense of purpose.

When we're burnt out, stressed out, discouraged, or bored, we can find ourselves unable to answer that all-important question: why do we do what we do?

Being able to answer it with certainty and confidence is crucial to our well-being. We're calmer and better able to cope with life stresses, and we live longer. Research proves it.

But what happens when the answer to that question—What's your purpose?—suddenly becomes unclear?

I tell my clients, "Look to your strengths."

Knowing what you're good at and why is incredibly validating as you navigate careers and relationships. I experienced this once when talking with my own coach, Whitney Johnson, about my desire to better position myself and my coaching business.

She encouraged me to take a second look at my StrengthsFinder report, a personal assessment that helps people identify the things they're good at.

I took the test for the first time five or six years ago, before I became a coach. My greatest strengths? Empathy, Connectedness, Responsibility, Arranger, and Activator.

Returning to these results felt so good. I viewed them from a different vantage point than when I first took the test, but it reconfirmed this: I'm doing exactly what I should be doing.

Another way to uncover your talents is to ask yourself what compliments you often receive. Do people cherish your high energy? Do they praise your ability to listen and relate to their problems? Pay attention to these descriptors—and let them substantiate what you do well.

Finally—and I find this thought particularly fascinating—consider what you loved to do as a child. What you did then (when you were simply doing based on curiosity) almost always says something about what you'll love as an adult.

I had a penchant for getting involved in student council, befriending the new kids at school, and falling into deep conversations with close friends on the trampoline. These are skills I still use regularly.

I recently took a tour of a Montessori school, and a teacher there confirmed this theory. She said she can often predict what a student will become—architect, artist, engineer—based on what interests them as a child.

Consider what you loved to do as a child. Ask yourself what compliments you receive. And if you want to go even further, try StrengthsFinder. However you do it, identify your strengths.

Your purpose, then, should come into focus.

Come Sail Away

Rooting women on is exactly why I do what I do.

When I made my leap to coaching, I wasn't old enough, or unpregnant enough, or with a trust-fund account to fall back on. But for years, I had served as an unofficial coach to dozens of friends, colleagues, and even bosses. Mine was the office people snuck into and asked for help figuring things out. Mine was the phone that people texted late into the night when life got too heavy to bear alone. Mine was the advice people sought over coffee or lunch or drinks or flights.

I was gifted exceptional listening ears. Good intuition. The ability to connect. A deep well of empathy. A sense of humor. A genuine desire to see others succeed. And the energy to help women build their wings—and then cheer them on as they fly.

So what if I wasn't yet forty?

My rule-breaking paid off in freedom, in fulfillment, and in joy.

I've gotten to coach women from California to New York and from Nationwide to Nike. I've coached them through promotions, through office politics, through negotiating raises, through career changes, through divorces, through parenting, through cross-country moves, through building businesses, through life.

I don't have the Sunday Scaries. I've integrated work into my life in a way that feels organic and whole and good, not restrictive.

I find immeasurable happiness in doing this work. And it's not just because it gives me the opportunity to manage the life I want (breakfast every morning with the girls, an office I can walk to, yoga at 11 with my favorite instructor, and the ability to control my travel schedule, among other things). It's because the work itself is magic.

I recently coached an intimate group of women through an eight-week course, including Claire, a woman who lives in the Carolinas. Claire is a single working momma with sole custody of her kids. One suffers from an eating disorder, and the other is battling mental illness. Life is challenging. Even her daughter's doctor suggested Claire find a way to spend money on herself for a little happy relief. Sailing, Claire shared, is what lights her up. But she could only sail when she borrowed a boat from her father or boyfriend.

During one morning session, as we all discussed what brings us joy, Claire looked at us from her computer screen, the Carolina sun shining brightly behind her. She told us she was making it her goal to buy her own sailboat. She didn't want to be dependent on others' permission or schedules to pursue her passion. It may take years, she said. But she was promising herself, with us as her witnesses, that she would do it.

"I need this," Claire confided, "for me."

I acknowledged her goal with a smile.

"You deserve that," I said.

Four days later, a text from Claire pinged into my phone. It was four words.

"I got a boat!"

Tears welled in my eyes.

This is what everything in my life was building toward. The wonderful jobs and the terrible jobs. Lessons taught gently by brilliant mentors and lessons learned the hard way. Personal failures (I am genuinely sorry, Mark) and personal victories (what a thrill that I get to date you forever, Nick).

Getting to use my strengths to help other women, other mommas, other humans—getting to help Claire find her sailboat—is why I was put on this Earth.

Recently, as I gave a virtual keynote, I talked about how guilty I felt when my kids had McDonald's three days in a row. We were temporarily moving homes for a renovation, during a pandemic, with my husband crippled by knee surgery, and I simply couldn't pull off getting my kids healthy eats. It was the best week of my kids' life. Yet I still felt guilty, I told the audience.

A mom from San Diego chimed in. She feels the same about serving Uncrustables to her kids, she said. She is fully capable of making PB&Js. But there is something so easy about tossing a few Uncrustables into their beach bag. Her kids love 'em. It saves her time. But there she is still, a working momma prioritizing quality family time with her kids, yet she feels shame every time she pulls those Uncrustables out of her bag.

So we talked out the shame game.

You see, the rules of parenting—these mystical rules we didn't create or agree to, yet somehow feel compelled to live by—are just like the mystical rules of womanhood and, really, the mystical rules of life.

They guilt us into feeling lesser-than for occasionally feeding our kids through a drive-through or from a box of frozen PB&J sandwiches, despite the fact that on top of working full-time, we spin them fresh smoothies every morning and nourish them with homemade recipes most nights. They trick us into spending all of our money on our families, suppressing our own happiness in the meantime, because a sailboat would be nothing but a selfish splurge. They convince us to stay up all night to impress the five-year-olds with the sweet treats because we must always prove our worth. They convince us to apologize for falling in love with a woman because that's not what's supposed to happen next. To marry the nice Catholic boy because he asked, and you wouldn't want to hurt his feelings now, would you? To run a hundred miles an hour on our hamster wheels, simultaneously overwhelmed and underwhelmed, shoulding the shit out of this precious gift we call life.

So, ladies, fuck the rules.

Because you can't sail off into the sunset without your own damn boat.

DEFINE YOUR OWN SUCCESS—THEN RELISH IT

A client of mine decided to accept a new job that would allow her to work fewer days each week so she could spend more time with her kids.

But instead of celebrating, she was worrying.

She fretted that given her new, shorter workweek, people may not take her seriously. Meanwhile, the career of her close friend in the same field was quickly advancing up the corporate ladder (long hours, big paycheck, positive attention), and it was stirring up some envy.

But wasn't this my client's choice? Yes.

So why was she still unhappy? She didn't stop to redefine success.

Comparison is, indeed, the thief of joy. And one of the key ways I know clients need to redefine their meaning of success is when I see them caught in the comparison trap. They're often measuring success based on an old metric, outdated goals, or arbitrary societal standards—money, accolades, power. They see others "succeeding" by this definition, and that thief of joy makes its move.

I've been there. As an example, there's no shortage of coaches touting life-changing retreats in Bali, Paris, and other grand places. It sounds exotic and fun. *Should I be doing what they're doing?* I ask myself. But the reality is I don't want to travel for weeks, leaving behind my family and lifestyle. Right now, that's not *my* idea of success. So long as I'm using the right measuring stick, I can easily reset—and celebrate that I'm right where I want to be. You can, too.

If you find yourself caught in the comparison trap, I encourage you to define what success means to you by asking yourself these three questions.

What does success look like for me in the coming year?
What do you want your life to look like one year from today?

One of the most helpful ways to answer this question is by evaluating the eight areas of the life wheel: family, work, money, personal growth, health and wellness, spirituality, community, and living environment. Choose your top three. How can you better commit yourself to those three areas over the next twelve months to honor what you've now established are priorities? Measure your success accordingly.

I do this each year to recalibrate my own definition, which helps me prioritize and take intentional action going forward.

What does success look like for me in the coming month?
Consider some smaller steps you can take toward your one-year goals.

For parents, success might mean making it to your child's school performance—with no late-night work on deck—to truly enjoy the event and celebrate with dinner afterward. Or perhaps, if you're hoping to make a professional change, success this month could mean sending an email to one of your career-crushes—someone you admire professionally—and requesting a call or coffee to talk. Maybe it's simply getting to one yoga class a week all month.

Whatever it is, make it realistic and concrete.

What does success look like for me today?
Seemingly small, intentional actions add up to significant changes. Think about one you can take today that will make you feel successful.

After spending years climbing the corporate ladder, my client may not stop wrestling with career envy overnight. My advice to her?

Remember your why—and remember what your measuring stick looks like. She wanted more time with her kiddos. So if she gets to read with them before tucking them into bed tonight, today was a success.

It's important to remember that your needs and dreams will change and evolve, so your definition of success will, too. If you try to apply just one definition to your entire life—or even just your entire career—you will be unsatisfied.

Push yourself to redefine success. Use your own measuring stick to analyze how you're doing. And don't forget to celebrate your victories along the way.

This Is It

On that beautiful fall afternoon so many years ago, when I was stuck in that windowless conference room on that four-hour call, I didn't want to choose; I wanted to change. So I took the next best step—right out the door.

I didn't have much of anything figured out. But I could see the spot where I needed to place my left foot in front of my right, and so I did it. And in doing so, I rewrote the story of my life. Now, I get to help others rewrite theirs.

Would you believe I still walk that same sidewalk every day? I do. Now, instead of taking it from a world-class marketing firm I despised to a condo where I lived alone as a confused divorcée, I take it from my own office to a beautiful, old brick house, where I sing and dance and giggle with little girls I adore, and where I enjoy wine on the patio with the love of my life.

I've face planted many times along the way. But I embrace every trip and every scar. Because it has led me here, to a place where I live life on my own terms.

This *is* it. And it isn't perfect. But it is bliss.

Life's greatest honor, I believe, is to be exactly who you are.

So step off the hamster wheel. Silence the noise. Sit quietly with the woman in your soul who is the one and only you there ever will be.

That woman—that unique, powerful, beautiful being—is not just enough; she is everything. And until you are true to her, happiness will be but a dream.

You owe it to you to be exactly who you were born to be.

So ladies, let me be clear: Trust your gut. Shed your shoulds. Prioritize, evolve, and repeat. Ask for what you need. Give yourself a break. Get out of your own way. Embrace the now. Always take the next best step.

And above all, let your heart be boss.

Acknowledgments

Nick, thank you for that first meeting at the Rossi and all that would follow. Your love is the best I've ever known. *Heart Boss* couldn't have been written without our story.

Mom, thank you for leading by example. Who would have guessed the kid you recorded all those spelling words for would someday write a book? Maybe only you. Thank you for believing in me even when I didn't.

Siblings, being born last into this crew is the gift that keeps on giving. (I mean, most days, at least.) There is no group I'd rather dominate a community bike race with than you.

Kristy Eckert, you are my right-hand woman, and I wouldn't have it any other way. You are so much more than a business partner; I consider you a sister. I love you.

Carrie Hay, the front porch meeting with the green pocket folder was the beginning of one of the most trusted partnerships I have ever had. Thank you for saving my ass time and time again.

Joel Showalter, you and your green pen make me look like I understand grammar rules. (I don't.) I am beyond grateful.

Joy Sullivan, you take my breath away each time I read your poems. Thank you for honoring my clients and me with your gift of words.

Friends, clients, and readers, my greatest honor is supporting your dreams. Thank you for inviting me into your lives.

I have and always will root for each of you fiercely.

About the Author

Regan Walsh is an executive coach and life coach who finds joy and fulfillment in helping women worldwide lead lives that sizzle.

She has worked with individuals and organizations from creatives at Nike to analysts on Wall Street and has been featured by media outlets nationwide, including *Forbes*, *Harvard Business Review*, *Fast Company*, and more.

Regan's own journey has been fraught with self-inflicted stress and unsatisfying busyness. Thankfully, it's also been a journey of intentional searching and incredible transformation. Prior to coaching, Regan spent fifteen years working in corporate, nonprofit, and creative agencies. She earned her executive and life coaching certificate from New York University and enjoys a fulfilling career as a coach, speaker, and writer.

Life's greatest honor, Regan believes, is to be exactly who you are. And whether that's a go-getting executive, a tenacious small business owner, or a lively stay-at-home mom, Regan helps women realize who that person is and how to be true to her. The result is not just happiness; it's contentment.

Learn more at *reganwalsh.com*.

A Gift for You

Want more? I've created a guide with exercises, writing prompts, and more so you can workshop your way to living life on your terms. Download your *Heart Boss* kit for free at *heartboss.com/gift*.

CPSIA information can be obtained
at www.ICGtesting.com
Printed in the USA
BVHW080235250921
617232BV00002B/165

9 781544 518725